CLASH OF ARMS
The World's Great Land Battles

CLASH OF ARMS

The World's Great Land Battles

Richard Garrett

Galahad Books
New York City

Foreword by Alun Chalfont

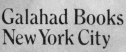

Library of Congress Catalog Card Number: 76-9452
ISBN 0-88365-362-1

Printed in Great Britain by Cox & Wyman Ltd.,
London Fakenham and Reading
Published by arrangement with Weidenfeld and Nicolson,
London, England

CONTENTS

Foreword

by Alun Chalfont

It is important to recognize that war is an art, not a science. Simply to advance that proposition is to beg a large number of questions. It is, for example, possible to argue that war – the use of organized violence by sovereign states in pursuit of their national interests – is immoral and indefensible; and that in the age of nuclear weapons its destructive potential is so great that it has become obsolete as an effective instrument of policy. Whether these arguments are valid or not, the study of war is one of endless fascination. Indeed, as Basil Liddell Hart recognized, it is essential to the preservation of peace. Yet that study, if it is to be constructive, should not be based upon scientific theory. Sir Brian Horrocks, one of the most distinguished battlefield commanders of the Second World War, once said that he had never understood any military theory – another way of saying that theorizing about war is a waste of time. Field-Marshal Radetsky put it another way: 'War is manifestly an art, not a science, an art by which, as is true of all arts, the sublime cannot be taught.'

One of the most profitable areas of study in the military art is that of actual battles, and the commanders who took part in them. Weapon systems change; equipment changes; but two aspects of war have certain immutable characteristics – strategy and tactics. They have both been variously defined, but a serviceable definition is that strategy is the art of conducting a campaign, while tactics is the art of conducting a battle, or part of a battle. This leads to the distinction which is often made between the great military commanders of history, like Alexander the Great, Wellington and Marlborough, and the outstanding battlefield generals, like Allenby, Montgomery and Wingate. The really great commander must understand the great sweep of strategy, 'the divine part of war' – and the broad, political context within which a particular campaign or battle is being fought; to be a supreme tactician is not enough.

The study of war cannot, of course, ignore the development of weapons and equipment – the invention of gunpowder which paved the way for projectiles of great range and rapid fire-power; the replacement of cavalry by artillery as the determining factor in battle; the impact of the steam locomotive and the internal combustion engine on the problems of logistics; the invention of the tank, still supreme on the modern battlefield; the introduction of the aeroplane; and, of course, the revolutionary impact of the atomic weapon and the missile which is now its principal delivery system. These great technological advances have immensely complicated the business of administration and supply and made mastery of the *Materialenschlacht* one of the most important, if not the most glamorous, of the arts of war.

Yet, behind all this, lies the most important factor of all – the human factor; and the real history of war is not that of tactics, or weapon systems or equipment; it is the history of the courage, resolution and steadfastness of soldiers; of the inspiration and imagination of their leaders; and of the battles which they fought together.

1 The Time and Tide had to be Right

Hastings 1066

William's invasion force embarked at the French port of St Valery. All told, about eight thousand troops were involved. During the next twenty-four hours, they would be at the mercy of the wind. In the event, they crossed the Channel at a speed of four knots.

Edward the Confessor (1042–66) had died without leaving an hereditary heir. William, the illegitimate son of Robert, Duke of Normandy (otherwise known as Robert the Devil), asserted that Edward had promised him the throne. Furthermore, he alleged that Harold Godwinson, son of the Earl of East Anglia and ruler of Wessex, had pledged himself to support the Norman claim: but, within a week of Edward's death, Harold had seized the throne for himself. From that moment, an invasion by William seemed to be inevitable.

Harold had no doubts about this. Throughout the summer of 1066 his small fleet patrolled the Channel, and he established a headquarters on the

Isle of Wight. By the middle of August, however, Harold's sailors were running short of food, and their vessels were in poor condition. They were ordered to London to refit. William could now send an armada across to England without any fear of opposition. As if to make things even more favourable, Harald Hardrada, King of Norway, decided that he, too, would contest the English throne. In mid-September, he landed an army at the mouth of the Humber; by the 20th, he had taken Scarborough, sacked Cleveland, and had reached Stamford Bridge, seven miles from York.

But Harald Hardrada's run of good fortune had come to an end. King Harold had hurried north with reinforcements; the Norwegians were put to the sword and vanquished. When the killing stopped, Harald Hardrada lay dead; of the three hundred ships that had sailed to England, only twenty-seven returned to Norway.

The Norwegian invasion had cleared away the last obstacle in William of Normandy's path. Two days after the Battle of Stamford Bridge, his fleet of six hundred transports and twenty-eight war galleys made a landfall at Pevensey in Sussex. The troops were put ashore without opposition; for the next two weeks, they ravaged the Sussex countryside – killing, burning, and looting.

The two main antagonists at the Battle of Hastings were in marked contrast to each other. Harold was six years older than William: a thickset, stocky

The Norman invasion force landed at Pevensey in Sussex. Later, William built a castle there – for fear, perhaps, that other European powers might follow his example.

individual of proven military ability. His stamina was considerable, his courage unquestioned. According to his own assessment of himself, he was a fighter of subtlety, a general who might be expected to spring a few surprises on his foe. In this respect, unfortunately, he was wrong. William – a taller man with thinning black hair and twirling moustaches – had already devised a revolutionary approach to military strategy. Harold might be content to assemble his men in close formation, to win an engagement by sheer brute and bloody strength. William had other ideas. In a sense, his tactics at the Battle of Hastings foreshadowed the days of artillery and, much later, tanks.

As if to make things more difficult for Harold, the English king misread his enemy's mind. William, he decided, would expect him to hurry south from Stamford Bridge and station his soldiers at the approaches to London. What, then, if he were to continue his forced march into Sussex, to bring the Normans to battle where William was least likely to expect it? There were disadvantages, to be sure. His troops would be tired; reinforcements expected from Northumbria and Wessex could not possibly arrive in time; William's men would be close to their supply ships, jubilant after two weeks of helping themselves from a subdued countryside, and well recovered from their

ABOVE The arrival of Harold's army was reported to William by scouts, who had observed outposts on top of a hill named Telham. The day was 14 October 1066; the time, about six o'clock in the morning.

OPPOSITE The face of William the Conqueror appears on this silver penny minted in about 1068.

11

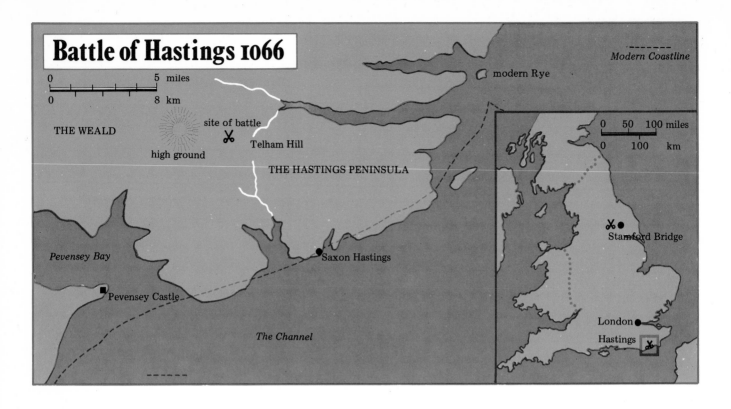

Battle of Hastings 1066

Modern Coastline

0 — 5 miles
0 — 8 km

THE WEALD

site of battle
high ground ✂ Telham Hill

THE HASTINGS PENINSULA

modern Rye

Pevensey Bay

■ Pevensey Castle

● Saxon Hastings

The Channel

0 — 50 — 100 miles
0 — 100 km

✂● Stamford Bridge

London ●
Hastings ✂

---

twenty-four-hour voyage across the Channel. But, to Harold's way of thinking, these matters were a small price to pay for that most precious of military advantages – surprise.

The road from London to Hastings lay through the great forest known as *Andredesweald* (nowadays the Weald). Presently, about seven miles from the coast, the trees cleared, and they came out into open country. It was now 13 October. The march from London had taken the better part of two days.

Harold had chosen his position with a shrewd eye. A hill, about a mile long, bisected the road. Behind it, the ground fell away sharply towards the edge of the forest. In front there was a comparatively gentle slope, but on either side it was considerably steeper. Infantry would find it hard to approach from the flanks, cavalry impossible. At the highest point on the ridge, about 275 feet above sea level, there was a hoar apple tree. Earlier history gives several other examples of such a tree being used as the rallying point for soldiers. In this instance it had two practical virtues. Its position ensured that the troops would have a clear view of Harold's two standards, the dragon of Wessex and his personal flag (always referred to as the Fighting Man). For his part, it would give him the best possible view of the battlefield. As a command post it could not be bettered.

If that impetuous hero King Harold imagined that the sudden appearance of his army would take William by surprise, he was to be disappointed. William was cool-headed, devious, and he had an astute awareness of that essential of all military engagements – intelligence. His spies and his scouts had been busy. He knew about Harold's movements, and it did not require any great feat of deduction to realize that he would take up this position. Apart from its tactical virtues, it was as if the ridge had been designed to block the entrance to the forest – and the road to London. His only problem, and it was not a difficult one, was to bring the English to battle before they had time to build defences. In this, as in almost everything, William was prepared. He had already worked out his order of march, and his strategy. It was merely a question of briefing his commanders, assembling his

12

men, and covering the seven miles that separated him from the English.

Of the two armies, Harold's may have been marginally the greater. All told, according to most estimates, it amounted to about eleven thousand men. The force under William's command added up to approximately eight thousand, but it was *different*. Within that total there were a thousand archers, three thousand horsemen, and four thousand infantry. They were well armed, and most of them were protected with iron helmets and mail shirts.

By contrast, Harold had no bowmen and no cavalry. His troops were armed with clubs, axes and short iron swords. Most of them were wearing their everyday attire; their only personal safeguards were kite-shaped shields. For want of any earthworks or palisades, these shields now had a doubly important role. With warrior pressed against warrior, each with his shield in front of him, they formed, so to speak, a wall. Once this protective screen had been pierced, there were no more obstacles.

In terms of morale, there was little to choose between the two armies. Harold's men were tired after the forced marches and campaigning of the past few weeks. But against this could be set the fact that they were bitterly angry about the Norman depredations in Sussex. These warriors were intent on revenge, and the only measure of it would be a heavy toll of Norman blood. A great many of them would not live to see it exacted, but this did not matter. No general expected victory without enormously heavy casualties; nor did Harold's troops go into battle without a sense of fatalism. A man was a fighter, and a fighter must expect to die. It was as simple as that.

William's army, on the other hand, had a much greater sense of professionalism. Their leader had little but scorn for what he clearly regarded as a blood-thirsty rabble. In his harangue before committing his troops to combat, William asked: 'Is it not shameful, then, that a people accustomed to be conquered, a people ignorant of the art of war, a people not even in the possession of arrows, should make a show of being arrayed in order of battle against you?' Yes, the soldiers agreed, it was. In such a situation, how could they possibly lose? Everything seemed to be in their favour, and this included the weather. It had been an unusually warm summer; now, with autumn here, conditions were still mild and dry. Adverse winds might have pushed their invasion fleet back to Normandy. High seas might have made disembarkation impossible. Heavy rains might have made the ground swampy and the use of horses impossible. But the winds had been favourable; the rain had never come. The road to the English position was firm. The sun was shining; and, behind the shields that crowned the hill in front, lurked inept amateurs. The omens could not possibly be better.

William's troops were deployed in three columns, with an élite corps of Norman warriors in the centre. This stone effigy depicting one of them can be seen in the church of St Martial at Limoges.

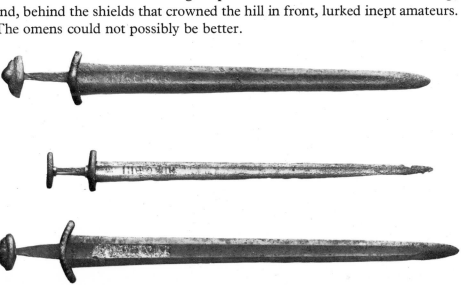

The English troops were armed with javelins, axes – and swords like these. But their most effective weapon was anger at the Norman depredations in Sussex.

13

INPRELIO

RIGHT The English position at
Hastings was on top of a hill named
Senlac. Since there had been no
time to prepare defences, the
soldiers' only protection was a wall
of shields.

BELOW The Norman army included
a force of three thousand mounted
troops divided up among the three
corps. In this scene from the
Bayeux Tapestry, Norman knights
and archers charge the 'human
wall' of Saxon infantry.

TRA:AN   GLORVM   EXER CIT

Harold's plan was simple. It was to hold the hill at all costs. His troops were massed in eight ranks along the length of the crest. The Norman soldiers would batter themselves to death against this wall of crudely-weaponed humanity. Then, when they ran out of thrust, when the line of attack faltered, the English would erupt from the ridge, pour down the slope in front, and drive the enemy survivors into the sea.

Duke William's ideas had more finesse. He had arranged his army in three groups. The centre, commanded by himself, amounted to about two-thirds of the force and was mostly made up of battle-hardened Norman veterans. On the left of the line, there was a force recruited from Brittany and Anjou led by Count Alan Fergent; on the right, a body of men from Flanders and the rest of France, commanded by Roger de Montgomerie.

It was within these formations, however, that William's brilliance as a general became apparent. Instead of hurling them haphazardly at the foe, he used a carefully thought-out strategy. First came the archers, armed with long bows and cross bows. When they were within a hundred feet or so of the enemy, they would unleash a barrage of arrows. Hopefully it would begin to soften up the resistance. Having fired their volley, they would withdraw. Immediately, the infantry would advance, fighting at close quarters and hacking holes in the opposition's ranks. After a while, when they became tired, they too would withdraw. At this point the horsemen would take over – charging through the gaps that the infantry had made, wheeling round at the rear of the position, creating havoc before they in their turn pulled back. At this point the bowmen were to advance once more, and so the cycle would continue over and over again – until the English had either been wiped out or else put to flight.

The Normans had left their base near the coast at about 4.30 that morning. A march lasting about four hours had taken them across the seven miles of rough country that lay between them and Harold's position. They formed up on a hill that capped the far side of a valley below the English front, put on their mail shirts, and waited with patience and resignation for the trumpets that would sound the advance. At some time between nine and ten o'clock on that fine October morning, William nodded an order. The trumpets translated his command into strident music. Stolidly, in an uneven line, the archers of the three groups moved forward.

A blind man could have seen the battle in his mind's eye simply by listening to the sounds. First there was the swish of a thousand arrows cleaving their way through the air, the thump and the scream as one or another found a target. Then a pause, until minutes later the panorama of noise took on the aspect of a boiler factory. This, literally, was the clash of arms: sword against sword, the bite of an axe into an iron helmet, the sheer animal rage of one man in mortal combat with another. Then, once more, the pause, before the thump of horses' hooves took up the refrain until this, too, reached a climax in the clash of iron.

During the early stages, it seemed as if events were turning out in Harold's favour. On the left of the Norman line, the Bretons were wavering. Their attack appeared to have spent itself; with part of the force now cut to pieces, the living were departing over the bodies of the dead.

If the English had been content to enjoy this brief taste of success, to maintain line and safeguard the length of the ridge, the outcome of the day might have been different. But the English peasant soldiers were too elated.

They broke formation and hurried in pursuit of the demoralized Bretons. Isolated from the main force, they became an easy prey for the Norman horsemen, who wheeled round and cut them to pieces. The English flank was now exposed; and, even more to Harold's disadvantage, the episode had given William an idea.

When, later in the day, the situation seemed to be reaching a stalemate, he ordered the group on the right of his line to advance, falter, and then to feign a retreat. True to his expectations, the men on the other end of Harold's army broke ranks, running jubilantly after the Flemings, and yelling their warcries of 'Olicrosse' ('Holy Cross') and 'Godemite' ('God Almighty'). But God was not with them. When they were well out into the open, the Flemings suddenly spun round and fought, whilst simultaneously the Norman cavalry surged round to the rear and inflicted a fearful slaughter. Shorn of the men on its flanks, Harold's army now stood clustered in a thick mass around the command post; but the two standards were still bravely fluttering defiance in the gentle breeze, and the English resolution was far from broken.

For hour after hour the carnage continued. The volleys from the bowmen were becoming thinner, as the men used up their stocks of arrows. Usually they were replenished by supplies unleashed by the opposition – the only merit in Harold's lack of archers was that it denied the Normans replacement ammunition. But the infantry had their swords and their axes and their clubs and their javelins. Above all things, they still had courage and anger. Nor was the Norman cavalry running short of zest. At one point, a rumour ran through the Norman ranks that William had been killed. To disprove it, he took off his helmet and rode down the length of his army, cheerfully waving his mace.

William was a man who was vouchsafed moments of inspiration. His first had been the feint by the group on his right; his second was to order his archers to aim upwards, giving their arrows a higher trajectory. The result was that, instead of confining their targets to men in the English front rank, they now inflicted casualties in the rear. It was one of these shots that is thought to have wounded Harold in the eye.

The English king, contrary to legend, was not yet dead. But his army was badly mauled. The ranks were now clustered so close together that it was impossible to evacuate the wounded; indeed, in many instances, an injured man was unable to fall to the ground. Wedged between their comrades, the dead and the maimed remained upright in an unholy pantomime. It would not be long before there were more casualties than there were able-bodied men. Soon, surely, the day would have to end.

The Norman *coup de grâce* took place at about five o'clock. Twenty Norman knights rode into the assault, trying desperately to punch a hole in the human citadel of English might. Four of them survived and their target was easily found. Within seconds of the breakthrough, they were cutting King Harold to pieces with their swords. One of them, indeed, was in such a fury that he continued to dismember the monarch for some while after he was dead.

Harold lay slain. His two brothers had fallen to the Norman sword. Indeed, out of the entire English army, only two senior commanders remained alive. Norman casualties had been considerable, too; but now, as the October sun went down, it was all over. The survivors of the English army melted away into the darkness of *Andredesweald* where pursuit was impossible. William the Bastard was now William the Conqueror. The Battle of Hastings was over.

OVERLEAF Traditionally, Harold is said to have died from an arrow wound in the eye. In fact his eye-injury was not fatal. As shown in this fragment from the Bayeux Tapestry the English king (*fifth from left*) was finally cut down by a Norman knight. The pictorial footnote shows English casualties being stripped of their weapons and armour.

2 Rout of the King's Men

Naseby 1645

In 1066, the population of England had been about one and a half million. By the outbreak of the Civil War in 1642, it had become five million, half a million of whom lived in London. Aided by inventions, and inspired perhaps by William's examples at the Battle of Hastings, the science of soldiering had made progress – on paper, at any rate. The army was now divided into four sections: infantry, cavalry, artillery, and engineers. Unfortunately, it was less effective than this may suggest.

The foot soldiers were armed with pikes and matchlocks. At close quarters, the former were adequately effective. As ancestors of the modern rifle, however, the latter still had a long way to go. True to their name, they used up a great many matches (in one engagement, fifteen hundred men disposed of five hundredweight in twenty-four hours). They were inaccurate, virtually useless when it was raining or when the wind blew strong, and they had a tiresome habit of exploding – thereby blowing up the men who should have been firing them.

Cavalry units came in two versions. One was the cuirassiers, who wore breastplates and were armed with swords and pistols. The other, dragoons, was to all intents and purposes mounted infantry.

All one could say about the artillery was that they had guns. Since these weapons seldom managed to get the range right, and since they were badly built, they did small execution. As for the engineers, they were little more than a phantom corps, so few of them existed.

When Charles I set up his standard at Nottingham in 1642, the people of England were certainly not in a martial mood. They had become softened by years of peaceful prosperity, and they were loath to interrupt this pleasant pattern of life by becoming soldiers. Consequently the troops on both sides were mostly rogues, vagabonds, and pressed men.

By and large, the north and the west of England sympathized with the King, the east and the south with Parliament. Scotland was divided. The Duke of Montrose was an active supporter of Charles I; the Scottish parliament, predictably, encouraged their colleagues in England.

The turning point of the war has often been defined as the Battle of Marston Moor (1644). As a defeat for the Royalists, it was significant, but not decisive. More important were two spin-offs. One was that it drew attention to a forty-five-year-old captain in the Parliamentary horse, whose name was Oliver Cromwell. The other was that, despite their victory, it made the Roundheads aware of how *bad* their forces were. The result was the creation of the New Model Army, a band of warriors governed by discipline, temperance and the Bible. By the following summer, the New Model Army had become an extremely effective fighting instrument, and Oliver Cromwell – yeoman farmer and MP for Cambridge – had been appointed lieutenant-general in charge of the Parliamentary cavalry. The expertise of both were to be put to the test near a small town in Northamptonshire named Naseby.

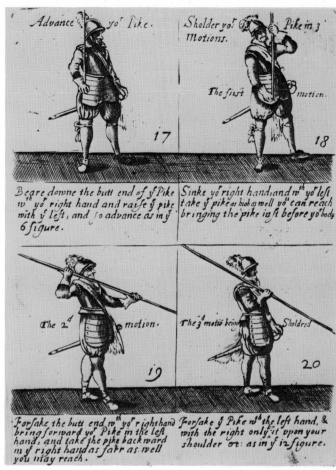

ABOVE Pages from a contemporary training manual showing the use of the musket and the pike.

LEFT In theory, the coming of artillery should have transformed the shape of a battle. In practice, its value was uncertain. Indeed, it is doubtful who was most afraid of the weapons – the enemy troops, or the gunners who had the unenviable job of firing them.

OVERLEAF Charles I dictates an order to his secretary in the field. One of the monarch's shortcomings as a general was that he found it difficult to make decisions.

One of the more tiresome characteristics of Charles I was that he found it very difficult to reach a decision. It was, then, something of a miracle that the Royalist and Roundhead forces ever came close enough to fight a major battle such as Naseby. In some respects the battle was an interesting example of English amateurism. For instance, when the two armies were drawn up ready to engage, everything was brought to a sudden standstill by the local hunt, which chased a fox across the space in between. At various points in the struggle, cattle sauntered on to the battlefield, and had to be driven out of harm's way by a farm worker. Nor were the casualties confined to soldiers – some of them were the ladies of Naseby, who had come to watch.

The commander of Charles's cavalry was his nephew, Rupert of the Rhine. In many respects, he was ideal for the role – tall, flamboyant, a man of considerable dash and courage. Unfortunately, there was one vital ingredient missing: judgment. Typically, when Prince Rupert first sighted a division of the Roundhead army, he drew entirely the wrong conclusions. Since they were going away from him, he assumed they were in headlong flight. In fact they were taking the very sensible precaution of moving out of sight. The result was that Rupert gave Lord Astley orders to pursue them. Since Lord Astley was commanding foot soldiers, and the Roundheads were riding horses, there was no action. The only outcome was that Astley's men, who had been occupying a good position, were now removed from it.

Reveille for the Roundhead army on 14 June 1645 was sounded at 3 a.m. By five o'clock, after a march of four and a half hours, the soldiers had assembled in Naseby. They ate breakfast; afterwards, from the foot of the market cross, one of the chaplains delivered the inevitable sermon. The text was taken from *Joshua* 22:22, '. . . if it be in rebellion, or if in transgression against the Lord, save us not this day'. Afterwards – refreshed, we must assume, in spirit as well as body – the men marched the mile and a half to what at ten o'clock was to become a battlefield.

Cromwell afterwards recorded his first impression on seeing the Royalist forces. 'When I saw the enemy draw up,' he wrote, 'and march in gallant order towards us, and we a company of poor ignorant men to seek out how to order our battle . . . I could not . . . but smile out to God in praises in assurance of victory.' No doubt the sentiments were very praiseworthy; as an example of accuracy, however, they were less good. There was little that was poor or ignorant about the New Model Army. It had something like thirteen thousand men in the field – compared with a paltry seven and a half thousand on the Royalist side. But what was even more important was its discipline and its professionalism. The dashing Prince Rupert was no match for a general of Fairfax's calibre. Cromwell was decisive; Charles was vague. When a man in the Royalist ranks was given an order, it was doubtful whether he would obey it. In a Roundhead unit, by contrast, he snapped to attention and carried it out at once. If anyone were seeking the Almighty's approval that day, it should have been Charles.

The country on which the battle was about to be fought was rough moorland, crinkled up into a collection of ridges. To say that the two sides faced each other across a valley is not strictly speaking true. The Royalists were set out in battle order for all to see; the Roundheads, on the other hand, were very prudently concealed behind a hill. Consequently, when the King's infantry began their advance, their first sight of the enemy was the sudden appearance of a line of warriors that seemed to grow out of the crest in front. Had the Roundheads' matchlocks been more technically accomplished

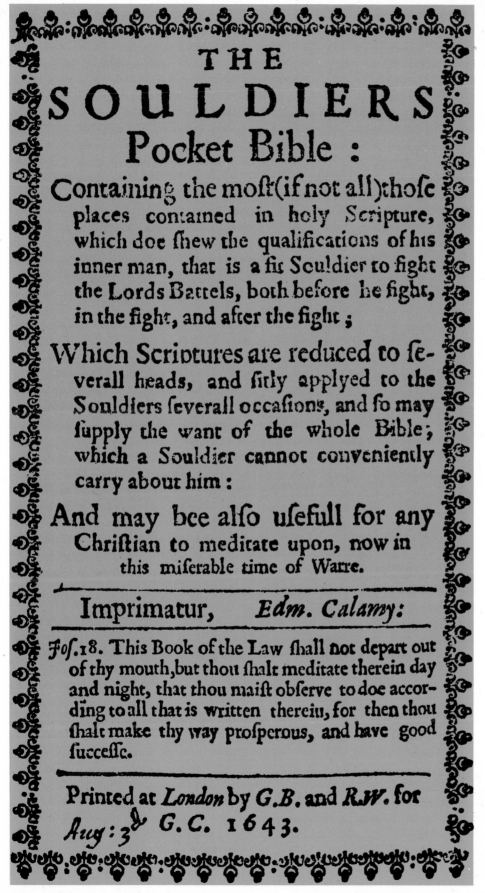

THE SOULDIERS

Pocket Bible :

Containing the moſt (if not all) thoſe places contained in holy Scripture, which doe ſhew the qualifications of his inner man, that is a fit Souldier to fight the Lords Battels, both before he fight, in the fight, and after the fight ;

Which Scriptures are reduced to ſeverall heads, and fitly applyed to the Souldiers ſeverall occaſions, and ſo may ſupply the want of the whole Bible; which a Souldier cannot conveniently carry about him :

And may bee alſo uſefull for any Chriſtian to meditate upon, now in this miſerable time of Warre.

Imprimatur, *Edm. Calamy:*

*Joſ.*18. This Book of the Law ſhall not depart out of thy mouth, but thou ſhalt meditate therein day and night, that thou maiſt obſerve to doe according to all that is written therein, for then thou ſhalt make thy way proſperous, and have good succeſſe.

Printed at *London* by *G.B.* and *R.W.* for *Aug: 3ᵈ* G.C. 1643.

The Bible was (or was supposed to be) the constant companion of soldiers in the New Model Army. Since the complete works were rather large for a man to carry with him on active service, a digest of the more pertinent passages was produced.

weapons, there might have been terrible execution. As things were, the few shots that were fired went wide of the mark.

Both sides were arranged in three divisions. On the right of the Royalist line was Prince Rupert and his cavalry; next to him there was Lord Astley with a force of infantry; and on the left was Sir Marmaduke Langdale, with more troops of horse. The King was at the rear. Cromwell faced Langdale on the right of the Roundhead line; Major-General Skippon was in the centre with, like Astley, a corps of foot soldiers; and General Henry Ireton matched horse with horse opposite Rupert. But, in addition to these dispositions, the Roundheads had two refinements that – either because there were too few men, or because they had not occurred to the Royalist generals (the more likely explanation) – were not to be found in King Charles's battle lay-out. One was the stationing of Colonel John Okey with a force of dismounted dragoons behind a hedge at right-angles to the field. It had the double advantage of enabling the men to enfilade the Royalist flank, and at the same

OPPOSITE In contrast to his opponent, Oliver Cromwell was shrewd and decisive. Some while before Naseby, he had made a reputation for himself as a cavalry general. Naseby was to show that it was well deserved.

LEFT Prince Rupert of the Rhine had plenty of dash and glamour, but lacked the cool-headedness essential in a good leader.

27

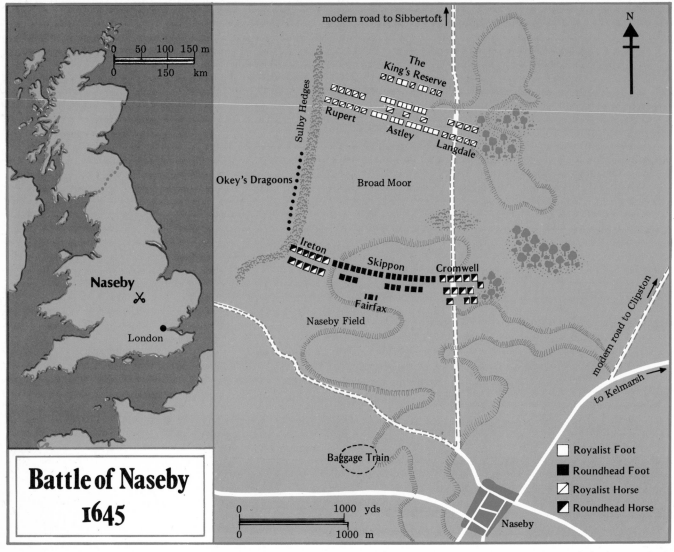

modern road to Sibbertoft

N

The King's Reserve

Sulby Hedges

Rupert

Astley

Langdale

Okey's Dragoons

Broad Moor

modern road to Clipston

Ireton

Skippon

Cromwell

Fairfax

Naseby Field

to Kelmarsh

Baggage Train

Naseby

□ Royalist Foot
■ Roundhead Foot
◩ Royalist Horse
◪ Roundhead Horse

0 50 100 150 m
0 150 km

0   1000 yds
0   1000 m

Naseby

✂

London

Battle of Naseby 1645

time to move them to any other part of the field where they might be needed. Similarly, Sir Thomas Fairfax, the Roundhead Commander-in-Chief, had stationed his cavalry force at the rear of the line as a mobile reserve.

At ten o'clock on this fine June morning, King Charles ordered his men to advance. The approach to the Roundhead positions was up a slope with the going made more difficult by the rough heathland. Bravely, though cursing and complaining, the veterans of Astley's infantry marched to meet Skippon's foot-sloggers. Since the latter had only recently been either recruited or impressed into the New Model Army, this was their first taste of battle. Whatever they may have had in the way of discipline and (possibly) enthusiasm was offset by lack of experience. When Astley's soldiers went in, fighting at close quarters with the butts of their matchlocks and with their swords, the Roundheads wilted and presently became a shambles.

Simultaneously, at the right of the Royalist line, Rupert's cavalry were giving a good account of themselves against Ireton's horse. At some point in this part of the engagement, Ireton noticed how badly things were going with Skippon's infantry. He wheeled round to render assistance; his horse was shot from under him; and he himself was wounded in the thigh and face, and taken prisoner. So far, so good. On two sections of the front, at any rate, the Roundhead pieces seemed about to be swept off the board. It was at this point that the impetuous Rupert made his fatal mistake. Instead of matching Ireton's move with a complementary tactic, he charged on ahead, leaving the battlefield behind and galloping into Naseby. When he called upon the Roundhead baggage train to surrender, the escort replied with a volley of well-aimed shots. Rupert's stampede for victory was over. He and his troopers were driven off and returned to the scene of operations – which, if the madcap prince had cared to think about it, was where they should have been all the time.

Rupert's departure was a disaster, for it exposed Astley's flank. Meanwhile Cromwell had been busy on the left of the Royalist line. After smashing through Langdale's horsemen, he wheeled round to the other flank and inflicted fearful punishment in the gap left by Rupert's ill-judged action. The Royalist infantry were now beleaguered on two sides by cavalry, whilst to their front Skippon's foot soldiers were being reinforced by Fairfax's mobile reserve.

The fact that the tattered remains of Langdale's units had now been driven into the arms of Rupert's returning warriors was of small importance. As the Roundhead forces closed in, the Royalist soldiers began to lose their taste for battle. One regiment after another laid down its arms; and when, at about this time, Rupert ordered a charge, his troopers refused to obey.

Whatever Charles I's faults may have been, nobody could have accused him of cowardice. When he saw how badly things were going, he decided to take a more active part in the battle. Since he had nothing more than one troop of horse at his disposal, it would have been an empty gesture. What was more, it would have amounted to suicide. Just as he was giving the command 'advance to the left', the Earl of Carnwath grabbed the bridle of the royal horse. 'Sir', said the Earl, 'will you go upon your death?' In the confusion, the word 'right' became substituted for 'left' in the order. Not that it mattered very much, for within minutes the Royalist army (or what remained of it) was in headlong flight. They did not rein in their horses until they reached Leicester.

BELOW LEFT Henry Ireton was a barrister by background. At Naseby, he commanded the Roundhead cavalry on the left wing. During the battle, he was wounded and captured, but later escaped.

BELOW Sir Thomas Fairfax, an inspired cavalry general, did as much as anyone to create Parliament's New Model Army. At Naseby, he served as commander-in-chief. At one point during the fighting, he personally captured a Royalist standard.

There is no accurate account of the Royalist losses that day, but it seems probable that a thousand were either killed or wounded, and five thousand taken prisoner. Among the victims was a small host of prostitutes who were captured with the Royalist baggage train. With a prudish fervour that can hardly be considered Christian, the Roundhead soldiers caused the Irish members (about a hundred ladies) of this small army of sin to be brutally bashed on their heads. The English whores, and there was no apparent reason for this distinction, had their faces slashed – 'in order', according to one writer, 'to render them for ever hideous.'

But Parliament's real gain from the battle amounted to even more than the destruction of an army: it lay in a collection of correspondence discovered in

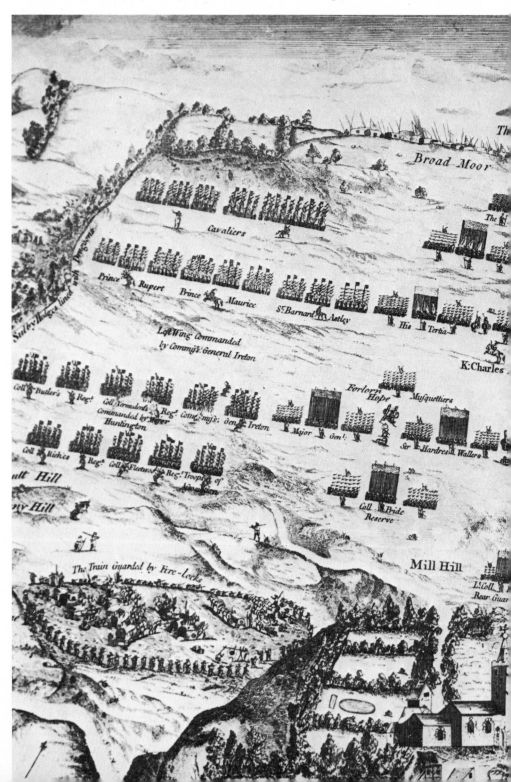

the Royal baggage train. These were letters from Charles appealing to various powers in Europe for intervention. Previously, the bulk of English people had been less than enthusiastic about the struggle. The King or Parliament – both were classed as that abstract entity 'them'. Only the pious money merchants of the City, and members of an emerging middle class – who doubtless hoped that one day they might become political nonentities – had shown any great concern for the Roundhead cause. But now everything was different. By inviting a foreign army to invade England, Charles had shown himself to be a traitor. This disloyalty to his own country was the ultimate cause of his defeat. It might have been better if the Earl of Carnwath had allowed him to make his final and pathetic stand at Naseby.

A contemporary view of the battlefield. The Roundhead baggage train was in Naseby itself. The armies were drawn up on rough countryside to the north of the town.

3 The Gap in the Line

Blenheim 1704

By the beginning of the eighteenth century, military innovations still raw at the time of the Civil War in England had matured. The science of artillery was now such that a confrontation could be preceded by a most punishing barrage. Engineers no longer existed only in name – they were skilful men who, among other things, could bridge a river in a surprisingly short time. As for the infantry, the matchlock had been thrown on to the scrap heap. The flintlock (which did not need matches) had arrived by this time; and the pike had been replaced by the bayonet. Nevertheless, foot soldiers still carried swords.

The system of infantry tactics was to march within thirty yards or so of the objective without firing a shot. At this point, the men discharged a volley. Using the smoke as cover, they charged – and the rest of the engagement was fought with bayonet, sword and butt. In this situation, the English soldier had few equals.

But the old soldiering virtue of brute force was no longer sufficient. The troops had to be better marksmen, and a higher standard of drill and discipline was required. Fortunately, at the outbreak of the War of Spanish Succession in 1702, a general of rare accomplishment was in charge of the British Army in Europe. He was a man in his early fifties; his name was the Duke of Marlborough.

During winter months, when the armies took a rest from campaigning, Marlborough worked his men hard. In platoons of fifty, they practised marksmanship on the range. They drilled as they had never drilled before, becoming more professional and more mobile. But this was not the sum of Marlborough's ability. He realized the importance of an efficient intelligence network and, no less vital, of a sound supply system. At the end of a long day's march, a soldier was able to rest. Food was brought to him in wagons (known as Marlbrouks), designed by the General for this very purpose.

During the first two years of the war, the English army had been mostly confined to the Low Countries. Elsewhere in Europe the situation had become serious. The French, with the Elector's consent, occupied Bavaria, which gave them a base for the threatened invasion of northern Italy; Vienna was menaced by an uprising in Hungary. The French army, under Marshal Camille Tallard, was cocky as became warriors who had not known defeat for over sixty years. There was, it seemed, only one way to set matters right. The idea was daring – some might have said impossible. The Allies would have to march across Europe from their bases in Holland, and bring the French to battle in Bavaria.

The operation that resulted from this idea was a magnificent example of a massive troop movement. Throughout the late spring and early summer, a long ribbon of redcoats tramped its way across the Continent. The men were always well fed and adequately rested. Whatever perils lay ahead, they were ready to endure them.

The French commander-in-chief,
Marshal de Tallard. His leadership
was muddled; his authority weak.

33

John Churchill
Duke of Marlborou

Marshal Tallard had encamped his army at a point where the River Nebel flows into the Danube from the north-west. It had the makings of a good defensive position. To the east, the flank was protected by the Danube and the village of Blenheim; on the west, around the hamlet of Lutzingen, rougher ground, steeper hills, and thick woodland would make an attack difficult, if not impossible. In between these two points, the Marshal had fifty-six thousand men. There was, he believed, little to worry about. Indeed, at seven o'clock on the morning of 13 June, he was writing to Louis XIV, telling him precisely this. Advanced units of the Allies had been sighted; but, according to his sources of information, they were about to retreat. He overlooked the fact that his crafty opponent, Marlborough, was apt to use agents to plant misinformation. Tallard was reacting just as the Englishman hoped he would.

Nor was Tallard prepared for the suddenness of the attack. The prelude to a battle was slow, even gentlemanly. It was very nearly a matter of the two sides tossing coins to see who would fire the first shot. But Marlborough had little time for the traditions of warfare. He intended to take the French by surprise. So far as such a thing is possible when you are handling fifty-two thousand troops, he succeeded. Tallard had just finished his report to the monarch, when an aide brought him a more accurate account of the Allied intention. He scribbled a hasty PS. Minutes later, the beat of drums and the call of trumpets told the Allies that the French were taking up their battle positions.

OPPOSITE The Duke of Marlborough, victor of Blenheim. Much of his success lay in his insistence that his troops be properly trained – especially in musketry.

BELOW The height of the conflict: three episodes from the Battle of Blenheim painted by Laguerre.

35

Tallard's plan was to post his infantry in Blenheim, Oberglau and Lutzingen – the three villages that stood on the crest of a ridge about seven thousand yards long. In the centre of this line, he massed his cavalry. With the Danube protecting one flank, and the rough country around Lutzingen guarding the other, his only serious concern was the area in front of his positions. But here, too, he was fortunate. The Allies not only had to cross the Nebel: their progress would be made yet more difficult by the marshy ground that extended from the river's banks. If everything went as the Marshal intended

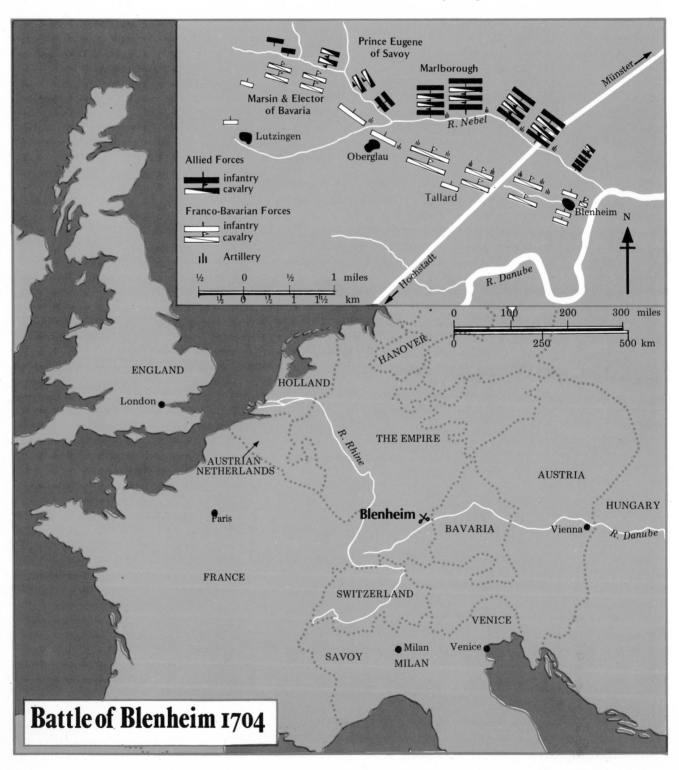

Prince Eugene of Savoy

Marlborough

Marsin & Elector of Bavaria

Münster

Lutzingen

R. Nebel

Allied Forces

infantry

cavalry

Oberglau

Franco-Bavarian Forces

infantry

cavalry

Blenheim

N

Artillery

Tallard

Hochstadt

R. Danube

½ 0 ½ 1 miles

½ 0 ½ 1 1½ km

0 100 200 300 miles

0 250 500 km

HANOVER

ENGLAND

HOLLAND

London

THE EMPIRE

AUSTRIA

HUNGARY

R. Rhine

AUSTRIAN NETHERLANDS

Blenheim

BAVARIA

Vienna

R. Danube

Paris

FRANCE

SWITZERLAND

VENICE

SAVOY

Milan

Venice

MILAN

Battle of Blenheim 1704

it should, the climax would come when his horsemen – the crack Gendarmerie – charged down from the ridge, supported by the fire of his foot soldiers in the three villages. Tallard himself intended to assume command over the troops between Oberglau and Blenheim; the Elector of Bavaria and Marshal Ferdinand Marsin were in charge of operations on his left.

In so far as Marlborough had a plan, it reflected his ability to think himself into the mind of his opponent. Tallard might well assume that the strong force of cavalry plus the squelchy ground at the front of the French line would discourage any attack from that direction. Despite the difficult terrain, the area around Lutzingen might seem to be more promising. Very well: if that was what Tallard expected, that was what he should have. Marlborough talked things over with his ally, Prince Eugene of Savoy – who commanded the Army of the Rhine – and an idea was born. Eugene and his Germans were to produce a diversion by assaulting the village of Lutzingen. The fact that they were unlikely to succeed did not matter. They would not only mislead the enemy, they would also pin down a sizeable sector of the French front.

At the same time, his own infantry would engage the garrisons at Blenheim and Oberglau. Again, it was not necessary to take these villages, but simply to contain the French soldiers and thus prevent them from doing serious damage to the English cavalry. This, roughly, was what Marlborough had decided before the battle began. What would happen afterwards was up to fate – or Tallard. The English general's flexibility was part of his genius. During an engagement, his aides and runners kept him exceptionally well

Blenheim village (*left*) was surrounded by a palisade. Marlborough's troops had been ordered not to fire until they could touch it with their swords.

Blenheim Palace in Oxfordshire. Designed by playwright-architect John Vanbrugh, it was Queen Anne's gift to her triumphant general.

informed of what was taking place. He moved from one trouble spot to another, giving precise, and usually effective, instructions on how to overcome the problem. He was ready to scrap one idea and replace it with another – and, in this respect at any rate, he had the edge of Tallard. Whilst Marlborough was fiercely independent, the French Marshal had been conditioned to rely on instructions from his King. Since the journey from Bavaria to Versailles was a long one, it meant that decisions took at least a week to arrive. Left on his own, Tallard was weak, indecisive, almost timid.

The worst part was at the beginning – those long hours when the Generals were setting out their pieces on the board. As if to prevent their troops from getting into mischief, they filled in the time by giving their gunners a little exercise. With fearful coordination, a line of cannon discharged its deadly burden of shot; the other side replied; and so it went on, minute by minute, hour by hour. While this was happening, the English infantry was wading across the Nebel, occupying the far bank, and then – waiting. There was so much to be done at the rear. The engineers had to build five bridges; the cavalry had to be brought across; and, just as important, Prince Eugene and his Germans had to hack their way into position for the assault on Lutzingen. All the while, the French artillery was smashing holes in the English ranks. At one point, Marlborough rode across no-man's-land in full view of the enemy to encourage his men. It was a brave gesture – and one that very nearly had an unhappy ending, when a French gun team scored a near-miss. At another, the General instructed his senior chaplain to conduct a church service. It would, he hoped, take the men's minds off their troubles; it might, perhaps, encourage the God of Battles to take sides.

It was now a few minutes after noon. The sun had climbed to the top of a flawless sky, and it was very hot. Marlborough's forces were all in their appointed positions; but there was still no news from Eugene, and there could be no beginning until the Prince was in position. At last a galloper arrived at the Duke's headquarters. Eugene was ready: the battle proper could begin. Quietly, Marlborough bade his senior officers: 'Gentlemen – to your posts.' The time was 12.30. The English infantry, accompanied by the rattle of drums, began to move forward.

Blenheim was surrounded by a palisade. The troops had been ordered not to open fire until they could touch it with their swords. At last there was the crash of a well-drilled line of flintlocks, and the crash of a scarcely less well-ordered reply. Brigadier-General Lord Rowe, who was commanding the assault, fell to the ground seriously wounded. A colonel and a major, who tried to drag him away from further harm, were both killed. All told, about two-thirds of the force was wiped out. Nevertheless, the action had been, in a manner of speaking, successful. The French commander, the Marquis de Clérambault, had been impressed by the English performance. Too impressed – for, without asking Tallard's permission, he pulled seven supporting battalions into the garrison, and then a further eleven that should have been kept in reserve. When he was done, twelve thousand men were jammed into this small village. There was scarcely room to move.

The English attacked again. Units of the Gendarmerie moved up from the flank to menace them. They were dispersed by Lieutenant-Colonel Francis Palmes who, riding at the head of five squadrons, put eight units of French horse to flight by charging them when their attention was occupied in another direction.

Meanwhile, at Oberglau, ten battalions under Prince Holstein-Beck had

been badly mauled. In particular, they had fared badly at the hands of a regiment of Irish mercenaries known as the 'Wild Geese'. The Prince was one of the first to fall; before long, the force was driven back to the banks of the Nebel. This might have been catastrophic. A hole had been cut on the right of the British centre. If Tallard had been quick enough, he might have poured his cavalry through the gap. But the Marshal seemed to be out of touch and the Gendarmerie wavered. There was time enough for Marlborough to ride on to the scene, sum up the situation, and send an appeal for help to Eugene.

Prince Eugene of Savoy, commander of Marlborough's Allies – the Rhine army. Louis XIV once said he was better suited for the church than soldiering.

39

Eugene was having a rough time of it, and he had no troops to spare. Nevertheless, he dispatched Brigadier-General Fugger with a regiment of imperial cuirassiers. The reinforcements smashed into the French cavalry and flung them back in disorder. By three o'clock that afternoon, Blenheim and Oberglau were both contained. What was more, de Clérambault had virtually neutralized all the French reserves.

Things were improving for the Allies. By 4.30, Eugene had managed to work his way around Lutzingen; one hour later, the main English advance began. With trumpets sounding, kettledrums beating, and their standards

fluttering high, two giant lines of cavalry spurred their horses into a quickening trot. The Gendarmerie panicked and fled from the field. A regiment of infantry that had been brought up to support them was cut down to a man, their corpses laid out in immaculate battle formation. With all the rest of his reserves bottled up in Blenheim, Tallard was done for. It was, as Marlborough proudly noted, 'as great a victory as has ever been known'. Vienna was safe. There could be no more thought of a French invasion of Italy. Marlborough had earned every stone that went into the building of Blenheim Palace in Oxfordshire – the gift of a grateful Queen Anne to mark the occasion.

The Blenheim tapestry, which hangs at Blenheim Palace, depicts the surrender of Tallard to Marlborough.

4 Keep the Powder Dry

Plassey 1757

India, and especially Bengal, was a hotbed of intrigue during the middle of the eighteenth century. There were large plots and small plots; but, in this labyrinth of double-talk, three characters stood out. One was Robert Clive, a servant of the East India Company, who had distinguished himself on the field of battle. Another was Siraj-ud-daula, the Nabob of Bengal – a tyrant of singular brutality, who was eager to prise loose the English grip on his realm. The third member of the trio was a character named Mir Jafar – one of the Nabob's generals who, with Clive's help, was planning to overthrow his master.

After months of indecisive engagements, innuendoes and broken promises, everything was working up to a climax. The time for talk was over; Clive and Siraj-ud-daula would have to fight it out. The scene of the conflict was to be Plassey, a town on the Hughli river's meandering course northwards from Calcutta. All told, the Nabob had something like fifty thousand men in the field, as against a mere three thousand soldiers commanded by Clive. To anyone else, the odds might have appeared to be atrocious; but Clive was not unduly perturbed. He had won earlier victories when the chances had seemed to be only marginally more favourable. In any case, he was doubtful whether Siraj-ud-daula could rely on his army. If Mir Jafar honoured his promise, a sizable part of it would transfer its allegiance to the English.

June 22, 1757, was a day of obscurity in more senses than one. To the troops of Clive's army, trudging northward along the wiggling line of the Hughli, the nature of the landscape was a matter of guesswork. Uncomfortably often, it was blotted out by deluges of rain that poured from the sky, accompanied by the crash of thunder and blinding tongues of lightning. Somewhere up in front there was a battlefield waiting to test their courage and skill. For the moment, the business of getting there was problem enough.

For Clive and his senior officers, the obscurity was of a more cerebral nature. They knew that, on the following day, a clash of arms with the Nabob would decide the future of the East India Company in Bengal. They also knew that victory depended on the conduct of Mir Jafar. The renegade general had promised handsome payment for the ruler's defeat – indeed, he had assured Clive that he could count on the support of a large part of the army. But, even more essential to Clive's peace of mind at present, he had promised to keep in touch. Time and again, the Englishman expected to see a runner carrying news from Mir Jafar, but nobody and nothing came.

Had something gone wrong? Had Mir Jafar changed his mind; or had the Nabob discovered the plot and put him to death? It was not impossible. As somebody had suggested, even private soldiers walking in the streets of Calcutta knew about it – down to the smallest detail.

At midnight, despite the bad weather, they reached Plassey. The river at this point bends itself into a shape like the letter U, thus forming a peninsula.

OPPOSITE Robert Clive, the victor of Plassey. Clive had received no formal training in the art of war. His skill as a military leader was instinctive, his tactics often highly original. At Plassey good fortune came to his aid by producing a rain storm when it was most needed.

43

The enemy was Siraj-ud-daula, Nabob of Bengal. Brutal, unstable and given to violent attacks of anger, he had been responsible for the Black Hole of Calcutta. At Plassey, his army was divided. Mir Jafar, one of his key generals, had promised Clive his support.

The defence of Calcutta depended on Fort William. It was here that the 'black hole' had been built to accommodate military offenders. The incarceration of (some estimates said) 146 Europeans in this small space began a chain of events that erupted at Plassey.

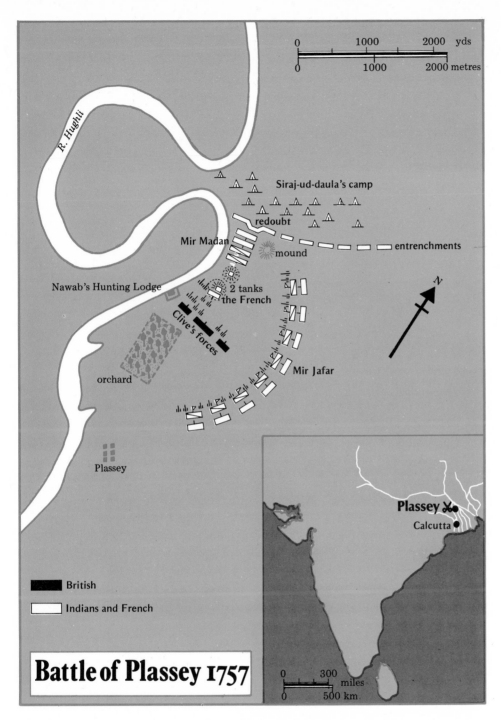

Battle of Plassey 1757

It was here, according to all reports, that the Nabob's huge army was waiting.

Plassey itself was only a small place. Its main feature was a hunting lodge owned by Siraj-ud-daula. Obligingly, it was unoccupied. Between the lodge and the river, there was a grove known as 'the Orchard of a Hundred Thousand Trees'. Since it measured eight hundred yards by three hundred, the name was something of an exaggeration. However, from a soldier's point of view it had the considerable merit of being protected on all sides by a mud-bank and a ditch.

At dawn on the following day, Clive climbed up to the roof of the hunting lodge. He could see the Nabob's army spread out in front of him – and, even to anyone so confident as he, it must have been a disturbing sight. All told, it

ABOVE Clive leads the attack at Plassey.

RIGHT A contemporary plan of the battle, showing the disposition of Siraj-ud-daula's forces. The British troops are drawn up in a grove on the left of the map.

OPPOSITE A Victorian artist's impression of the fighting at Plassey. Clive's troops are occupying a grove known as 'The Orchard of a Hundred Thousand Trees'. The Nabob's cavalry seem to be attacking; but, in fact, the battle was less spectacular.

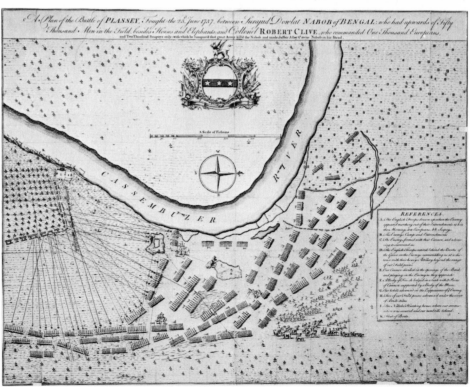

amounted to thirty-five thousand infantry, fifteen thousand horsemen, and fifty-eight tolerably large pieces of artillery.

The bulk of the army was still stored away in the U formed by the bending river. On the ground more immediately to his front, there was a battery of artillery that looked as if it was manned by about fifty Frenchmen. Over on the right, spread out in the shape of a half moon, and extending from the Nabob's camp to a point not far from the edge of the grove, the forces of Mir Jafar and another break-away general could be identified by their distinctive flags. They would be the source of victory or annihilation. The question was: which? There was still no word from this most enigmatic of men. Surely there should be *some* message?

Clive's plan was similar to those he had used on other occasions. With a mere three thousand men and ten light cannons, he did not stand a hope in a straightforward clash of arms. But this was not his method. He intended to remain where he was until darkness, relying on the defences of the grove to protect his troops from the enemy's artillery. After that, he would depend upon three fundamentals he had learned about Indian soldiers. The first was that their morale was lowest at night – in the majority of cases they simply lay down and went to sleep. The second was that they became useless if their leader was either killed or captured. Finally, they were liable to become panic-stricken when they were attacked from the rear.

Having assembled these observations, Clive formulated an idea. Once the sun had gone down, he would thrust his small army through the Nabob's

When an Indian ruler arrived for a battle, he travelled in suitable style. This nineteenth-century painting depicts Siraj-ud-daula's progress to Plassey. Before the following day was over, he had been deposed and was fleeing for his life.

lines with no thought for anything but speed. On the far side, they would turn about and hit the enemy from behind. Since the Nabob himself was unlikely to be anywhere else, he would be one of the first victims of the assault. After that, it should be a comparatively simple matter of mopping up those who had not already fled.

At eight o'clock, the French gunners opened fire. Clive's own men had been formed up in front of the grove – with the ten field pieces concealed behind some brick kilns over on the left of the line. Within half an hour, ten of his Europeans and twenty sepoys had been either killed or wounded. Such wastage could obviously not be allowed to continue. Leaving the artillery out on its own, he ordered the remainder into the cover of the grove.

For the next four hours, the two sides bombarded each other. At about noon, a few drops of rain fell from the now cloudy sky. They were the vanguard of another deluge; within minutes, everybody and almost everything were saturated. Since this included the Frenchmen's gunpowder, the opposition's cannon soon became silent. Prudently, Clive's men had kept their ammunition beneath the cover of a tarpaulin. The result was that the cannonade now became one-sided, but this fact seems to have escaped one of Siraj-ud-daula's most loyal, brave and popular generals – a man named Mir Madan. Apparently unaware that he could expect no help from his own side, and that he had everything to fear from the other, he broke cover with a squadron of cavalry and attempted to charge the English guns.

Poor Mir Madan – he was shot to pieces almost immediately. True to custom, once he had been disposed of, his surviving horsemen fled. It was, in a sense, the turning point of the battle. Mir Madan carried far more weight than the Nabob; now that he was gone, the spirit of the army died with him.

Clive had been drenched by the downpour. Whilst Mir Jafar was not doing anything to help, he was, at least, doing nothing to hinder. Deciding that events could look after themselves for the next few minutes, he went into the

Mir Jafar (*left*) did little to help Clive overthrow the Nabob as he had promised, but after the battle he gave the victor a vast sum of money. Here he presents Clive with a contribution to his fund for disabled soldiers.

hunting lodge to change his clothes. Before he had finished, however, an orderly rushed into the room to inform him that the fortunes of this small war had taken an unexpected turn. According to this man, Major Kilpatrick, the second-in-command, had suddenly gone into the attack. Since he should have been sheltering in the grove, Clive was furious. Without bothering to put on his coat, he stormed outside, caught up with the erring major, and promptly relieved him of his duties.

On calmer reflection, however, Clive decided that what had begun might as well continue. He sent word back for another officer to join him with more men, then he marched on towards the Indian lines. Over on the right, the great arc-shaped formation of Mir Jafar's division looked on with interest – rather like a crowd of spectators at a football match.

The Nabob's favourite put up a brief and unexpected show of resistance, but the gunners had done their work well. The shell that had shattered Mir Madan had knocked the life out of the army, and there was no fight left in it. By five o'clock, the Nabob had fled and the battle of Plassey was over.

On the following day, Clive sent a note to Mir Jafar. 'I congratulate you on the victory,' he wrote, 'which is yours, not mine.' He certainly did not mean it, and Mir Jafar must have been mad if he believed it. But who minded? The evil Siraj-ud-daula had been overthrown (he was later caught and murdered with fitting brutality); Mir Jafar paid Clive what can only be regarded as a fortune; and peace of a kind was restored to Bengal. As battles go, Plassey was scarcely an epic: on the English side seventy-two men were killed or wounded, on the enemy's about five hundred. But it had served its purpose, and that was enough.

Siraj-ud-daula's artillery, on its movable platform, drawn up against Clive's army.

49

5 Storming the Heights

Quebec 1759

As every schoolboy knows (to borrow a phrase used by Macaulay, Swift and a couple of others), a battle was fought on the Heights of Abraham outside Quebec on 13 September 1759. The two Commanders-in-Chief, Major-General James Wolfe and Lieutenant-General the Marquis de Montcalm, were both killed, and a crushing blow was dealt to French power in North America. But what every schoolboy may not have considered is the extra-ordinary time-structure of the affair. The Battle for Quebec was begun, reached a climax, and was over in less than an hour. The cost of British victory in terms of ammunition was one round per soldier; and, since the men fired in unison, the moment of truth lasted for less than one second. Nevertheless, it had required nine months to produce this critical instant in history; a large force of troops had been transported across the Atlantic; and the hardship and anxiety that preceded it made the British general so ill that he would probably have died in any case.

It was William Pitt who decided that the fall of Quebec must be one of his country's prime objectives in the Seven Years War 1759 programme. It was Pitt, too, who took the unorthodox decision of appointing James Wolfe to command the operation. At thirty-two years of age, Wolfe was comparatively junior. He was delicate; he had a reputation for eccentricity; and, on at least two occasions, he had been overlooked in the rat race for promotion. Never-theless, Pitt believed in him sufficiently to entrust this great undertaking to him.

The problem of taking Quebec was a difficult one. By midsummer, 1759, the British had occupied the Isle of Orleans downstream of the French stronghold. They had a foothold on the north bank of the St Lawrence, and they were firmly established on Point Levis, a headland on the far side over-looking the city. The ships of the Royal Navy now had the river to them-selves; and yet, despite all this, there remained the question of where and how to take the army across water, and to put it ashore at a point where it stood a reasonable chance of surviving.

Montcalm's army amounted to about seven thousand men, and there was obviously a limit to what he could do with them. The defences of Quebec itself were in a poor condition as the result of corrupt French officials, and shoddy workmanship by the builders who had led them astray. All this, you may say, added up to an impossible situation – one that did everything to favour the English. But Montcalm had a natural ally in the cliffs that flanked the river. They were so steep, he considered, that it would be impossible to bring troops ashore without incurring serious casualties.

As a good general should, Montcalm had attempted to decide what, if he were in Wolfe's place, *he* would do. The result of these deliberations was that he concentrated his forces to the east of the city, along a line that ended near a river named the Montmorency. True to the French general's thinking, Wolfe did try an assault from this direction. The battle, if that is not too

Although slight this is the most convincing portrait of Wolfe I have ever seen. Cf Schaaw prints. K. Wright. 1864.

to Isaac Barré
from his friend
Geo: Townshend

grandiose a name for it, took place on 31 July. A change in the weather, the uncertain tides, and a confusion of orders turned it into a fiasco. Wolfe would have to think again; he was, as he noted, confronted by 'a choice of difficulties'.

Precisely who decided that it would be better to make the attack at a point upstream is uncertain. History has given the credit to Wolfe, though it seems more likely that the idea was conceived by his three brigadiers, Townshend, Murray and Monckton. During the latter part of the summer, Murray carried out a raid on the enemy line of communication at a place named Deschambault. This, perhaps, was the key to everything. He had shown that it was possible to land men on the north bank of the river, to the west of Quebec.

The days before the decisive battle took place were attended by a good deal

Brigadier-General George Townshend devoted most of his artistic skill to lampooning his commander-in-chief, James Wolfe. On this occasion, however, he used his talents to more sympathetic effect.

of confusion. Wolfe was now seriously ill, probably suffering from rheumatic fever. He refused to take the brigadiers into his confidence, he was depressed almost to the point of defeatism. But, despite this, a plan was created; the troops were embarked on the ships; and everything – even to such details as the transportation of tents and blankets – had been arranged.

About two miles above Quebec, there is a cove named the Anse au Foulon. From it, a path runs up to the top of the cliff, leading to an expanse of flat tableland known as the Heights of Abraham. It would not be easy to make a landing there; indeed, at first glance, the idea seems to be crazy. How could an army, about four thousand strong, be disembarked on such a small beach; how could all these men, their guns and their supplies, be marched up a steep and narrow path on which only two men could travel abreast? Impossible! Even so, if something fairly close to a miracle could bring this about, the Anse au Foulon had a great deal to commend it.

The Heights of Abraham might have been designed by nature as a battlefield. If Wolfe arrayed his army across it, Montcalm would have to come and fight, for his supply line from bases up river ran right across the middle. And if the operation were carried out at night, if the soldiers were put ashore in secrecy, Montcalm would be taken by surprise. By the time he could bring his army from the far side of the city, Wolfe's men would be deployed in battle order and ready to fight.

The transports were anchored upstream of the cove. Round about midnight, the tide began to ebb, and this was a great advantage: it meant that the

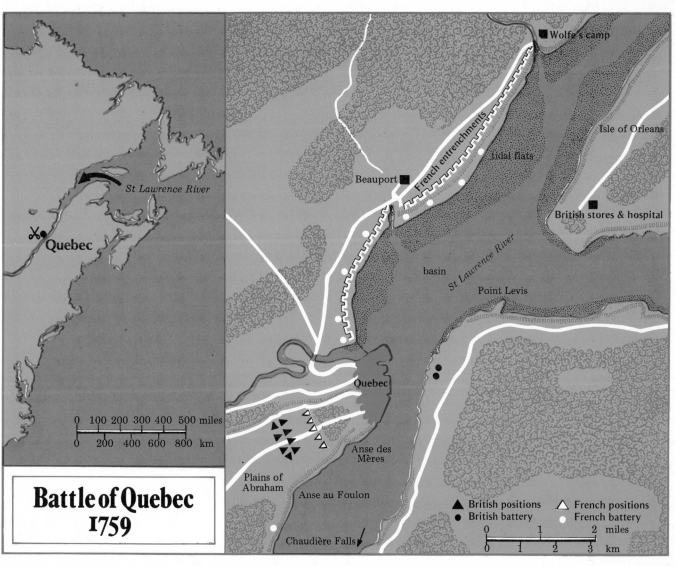

St Lawrence River

Quebec

0 100 200 300 400 500 miles

0 200 400 600 800 km

Battle of Quebec
1759

Wolfe's camp

French entrenchments

Beauport

Tidal flats

Isle of Orleans

British stores & hospital

St Lawrence River

basin

Point Levis

Quebec

Anse des Mères

Plains of Abraham

Anse au Foulon

Chaudière Falls

▲ British positions   △ French positions
● British battery   ○ French battery

0   1   2   miles

0   1   2   3   km

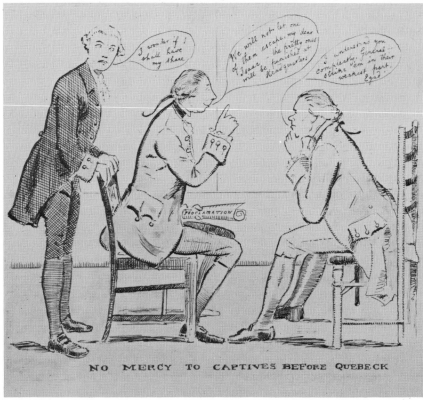

NO MERCY TO CAPTIVES BEFORE QUEBECK

landing craft would be carried towards the landing place by the current.
With little need to use oars, the journey could be conducted in silence. As an
extra bonus, the moon was in its last quarter. The darkness would make
navigation more difficult, but it would also ensure that the flotilla of boats
was unseen from the shore.

As a matter of fact, a French sentry did become aware that some vessels
were travelling down the river; but he mistook them for a convoy of supply
ships that was expected, and, beyond yelling a greeting, he took no action.

By 1.30 on the morning of 13 September, the first wave of landing craft
was under way. Forty-five minutes later, a second cast off from the transports.
The operation, for better or for worse, had begun.

To commit troops to battle requires a streak of optimism in the mind of the
commander. However desperate the circumstances may be, he must feel that
there is a possibility – even a probability – of winning. In this case, the landing
operation went as well as James Wolfe could have imagined. The soldiers and
the sailors carried out their roles perfectly. They made the journey to battle
in absolute silence; they easily overcame the small French detachment that
covered the path to the Heights of Abraham; they even managed to bring a
couple of cannons up the track. It was almost too easy. Indeed, the only man
who found any difficulty in reaching the cliff-top was James Wolfe. His illness
had left him in a badly debilitated condition, and he had to be helped.

At six o'clock, the black night dissolved in rain. But by this time the Plains
of Abraham were covered by a scarlet mass of British soldiery. Each man had
been issued with twenty rounds of ammunition, and each man was now looking anxiously towards Quebec. When would the French army make its
appearance? Would, some of them wondered, it *ever* come?

They need not have worried. Montcalm's first reaction had been to doubt
the messenger who brought him news of the British landing. It was, he said,

Return of the Killed, Wounded and Missing at the Battle of Quebec, September the 13ᵗʰ 1759.

Regiments	Killed											Wounded											Missing		
	Colonels	Lt. Colonels	Majors	Captains	Lieutenants	Ensigns	Adjutants	Qr. Masters	Surgeons	Mates	Serjeants	Drummers	Rank & File	Colonels	Lt. Colonels	Majors	Captains	Lieutenants	Ensigns	Adjutants	Qr. Masters	Surgeons	Mates	Serjeants	Drummers	Rank & File	Serjeants	Drummers	Rank & File
Major Genl. Jeffery Amhersts											2						4							5		52			
Lieut. Genl. Phillip Braggs				1				1			3						3	1	1					4	1	39			
Lieut. Genl. Charles Otways				1							6						2	4						1	—	28			
Major Genl. James Kennedys											3							1						2	1	18			
Lieut. Genl. Peregrine Lascelless											1						2	4	2					1	2	26			
Colonel Daniel Webbs																										3			
Colonel Robert Anstruthers				1							8						2	1	1					3	—	80			
Brig. Genl. Robert Moncktons				1							5						1	3	2					2	1	80			1
Colonel Charles Lawrences																										2			
Colonel Simon Frasers			1	2				1			14						2	3	3					7	—	131			2
Louisbourg Grenadiers				1							3							1	4						—	47			
Total			1	6	1			3			45						13	26	10					25	4	506	—	—	3

Royal Train of Artillery.

	Bombardiers	Gunners	Matrosses	Total
Killed		1		1
Wounded	1	1	5	7
Total	1	2	5	8

Regiments	Officers Names	Rank	Killed	Wounded
Major Genl. Jeffery Amhersts	John Maxwell Senr.			
	John Maxwell Junr.			
	William Allen	Lieutenants		Wounded
	Robert Ross			
	Ralph Cely			
	Kumb Milbank	Captains		Wounded
Lieut. Genl. Phillip Braggs	Thomas Spann		Killd	
	William Cooper	Lieutenants		
	William Evans			Wounded
	Paxton			Wounded
	William Henry Fairfax	Ensign		
Lieut. Genl. Charles Otways	John Maxwell			
	Luke Gardiner	Captains		
	William Maxson		Killd	
	Charles Gore			
	Richard Allen	Lieutenants		
	Gabriel Maturin			Wounded
Major Genl. James Kennedys	James Cockburn			
	Jones	Ensign		Wounded
	Gardiner	Captain		
	Brack			
	Gwynett	Lieutenants		Wounded
Lieut. Genl. Peregrine Lascelless	Elver			
	Henning			
	Seymour		Killd	
	Dunlop	Ensigns		Wounded
	Faunce			
	Vidal			
	Bird	Captains		
	Hemptin			
Colonel Robert Anstruthers	Grant	Lieutenants		Wounded
	Bainly			
	Pottinham	Ensigns	Killd	
	Samuel Holland	Captains		
	James Calder			
	James Safsey	Lieutenants		
Brig. Genl. Robert Moncktons	Alexander Shaw			Wounded
	Charles Cameron			
	William Snow Steel	Ensigns		
	Ross	Captain		
	Rory McNeil	Lieutenants	Killd	
	Alexander McDonnell			
	John McDonnell			
	Simon Frazer	Captains		
	Ranald McDonnell			
Colonel Simon Frasers	Archibald Campbell			
	Alexander Campbell	Lieutenants		Wounded
	John Douglas			
	Alexander Frazer Senr.			
	James McKenzie	Ensigns		
	Alexander Gregorson			
	Malcom Frazer Senr.	Lieutenant	Killd	
	Jones	Captain		
Louisbourg Grenadiers	Ochterlony			Wounded
	Nevin	Lieutenants		

General & Staff officers

Major Genl. James Wolfe — Killd
Brig. Genl. Monckton — Wounded
Col. Carleton Qr. Mr. Genl. — Wounded
Capt. Spital Maj. of Brigade — Wounded
Capt. Smyth Aid de Camp — Wounded
Major Barré A.g. Genl. — Wounded

Lieut. Benzell Engineer — Wounded

impossible. However, a short walk to the top of a nearby hill, a glance through his telescope, and he saw that the report was true. He ordered a detachment of sharpshooters to move round to the woods on the British left. The rest of the army formed up in threes and took to the road. At eight o'clock, a battery of guns on the west wall of Quebec opened up on the invaders.

James Wolfe had been pacing up and down abstractedly, a thoughtful frown on his pale, pointed face. The Heights of Abraham – a sizeable field speckled with bushes and shrubs – now seemed to be so large, and his army so small. What would Montcalm have done, what was he likely to *do*? Again and again, he returned to the questions; now and then he murmured an order to an aide, and minutes later a battalion moved into place. It was as if he were laying out pieces on a chessboard; but in this game there were no rules about where they ought to be.

The line, he decided, must be eight hundred yards long. Such a length was unreasonable, but he had no alternative. Consequently, the forward troops had to be strung out in two ranks instead of the more conventional three. Brigadier Monckton should command the centre; Murray should take up his station on the left; and Townshend was to take charge of the reserve. He himself would establish his command post on the right of the line. By 9.30 everybody was in position, and over in the direction of the city Montcalm's army could be seen approaching. His regular battalions were wearing smart white uniforms. Each had a unit of less elegantly clad militia attached to it.

When a general died in battle, it was considered fitting that his last moments should be recorded with drama and romance. The study of Wolfe's death at Quebec by Benjamin West (*opposite*) is notable for the fact that hardly anybody shown in it was present when the British commander died. Compare it with the more accurate portrayal of the same event on this page. As it indicates, only three other men were present – two junior officers and a grenadier.

It was still raining, and a light breeze had sprung up.

At ten o'clock, Montcalm gave the order to attack. A roll of drums signalled the advance, the colours were unfurled, and the Frenchmen began to cheer. They advanced at the double, expecting the British line to open fire at any moment. But the British did nothing. The French came on until they were a hundred and thirty yards away. Then they fired the first volley; but the stolid British infantrymen still did nothing. It was uncanny, frightening, to watch these men who stood so firm and fearlessly, and yet who took no action. The French moved forward again. One hundred yards, eighty yards, sixty yards, forty yards . . . Suddenly the British line exploded like a thunder clap. In what has been described as 'the most perfect volley ever fired on a battlefield', the men had unleashed a huge surge of destruction. One moment, Montcalm's force was an efficient body of fighting men; the next, their ranks torn to pieces by the musket fire, they were a dazed and frightened rabble. Within fifteen minutes of the battle's beginning, they were in full retreat, pursued by the thin lines of redcoats.

James Wolfe did not live to enjoy his victory. He never saw the inside of Quebec, for by the time the enemy was in full flight he was dead. After being hit in the wrist and the groin, he was finally struck down by a bullet that pierced his breast. His only companions during his moment of death were two junior officers (Lieutenants Browne and Henderson) and an anonymous grenadier. Everybody else was too busy chasing the French.

6 A Rabble Becomes an Army

Bunker Hill 1775 and Yorktown 1781

General Thomas Gage, Commander-in-Chief of His Majesty's Forces in North America.

Major-General John Burgoyne was one of three generals who arrived from Britain at the outbreak of the Revolution. He had a modest talent as a soldier and as a playwright; a genius for incurring debts. Later, he was to be defeated at the Battle of Saratoga.

The dispute of Great Britain versus the North American colonists centred around that fundamental of democracy: no taxation without representation. The colonists suffered a great deal of the former and enjoyed none of the latter. In 1770, after five Bostonians had been killed by British troops in a riot, Parliament conceded that there was something to be said for their argument. With a few strokes of the pen, all the taxes were repealed with one exception: tea. By maintaining a levy of this commodity, the Government reserved its right to resume the role of extortioner; it kept, so to speak, its options open.

American opinion was far from satisfied. In 1774, a number of Boston citizens, thinly disguised as Red Indians, threw the freight of a recently-arrived fleet of tea carriers into the harbour. The British Government's reply was to demand the payment of £15,000 to the East India Company by way of compensation. If it was not forthcoming, the port of Boston would be closed to commerce.

Predictably, the relationship between the colonists and the mother country became even more precarious. On village greens along the eastern seaboard, men turned out to practise drill, and supplies of arms were hidden away for use in a conflict that many of them believed would come soon.

In the spring of 1775, a detachment of troops was sent to Concord by way of Lexington to confiscate these hidden arsenals. Shots were fired: on the way back, the opposition was so effective that the soldiers had difficulty in regaining Boston. Nevertheless, the colonists continued to affirm their loyalty to George III. Their war, it seemed, was a private affair with Parliament.

General Thomas Gage, Commander-in-Chief of His Majesty's Forces in North America, had no doubts about the seriousness of the situation. An appeal to London for reinforcements produced a substantial number of troops and three more generals – William Howe, John Burgoyne, and Henry Clinton. Howe had led the Light Infantry that spearheaded Wolfe's ascent to the Heights of Abraham; Burgoyne combined soldiering with a small talent as a playwright and a considerable ability to incur debts; Clinton was a veteran of the Seven Years War in Europe.

The key to Boston lay on the far side of the Mystic River north of the town, the Charlestown peninsula. If the colonists established guns on it, they could wreak havoc among the naval ships in the harbour. They might even bombard the city itself. The peninsula must, Gage decided, be occupied without delay.

Led by such men as Israel Putnam (who had seen service with the British in the French and Indian wars), Colonel Richard Grundy (the engineer responsible for the transport of Wolfe's cannon to the Heights of Abraham), and William Prescott (he'd been offered a commission by the British, but conscience compelled him to refuse), the colonists had come to a similar decision. On 16 June 1775 – the day before a force commanded by Howe was due to make an assault on the peninsula – they occupied a knob of land known as Breed's Hill, and became busy building a fort.

LEFT In 1770 five Bostonians were killed by British troops in a riot. This was the beginning of hostilities between the colonists and the mother country.

OVERLEAF The attack on Bunker Hill and the burning of Charlestown.

BELOW LEFT Israel Putnam, commander-in-chief of the American forces, had fought with the British in the French and Indian wars. He exhorted his men to hold their fire until they could see the enemy's gaiters clearly.

BELOW In his attempt to recruit loyalists to the colours, General Howe relied on rhetoric – and promises.

TEUCRO DUCE NIL DESPERANDOM.

First Battalion of PENNSYLVANIA LOYALISTS, commanded by His Excellency Sir WILLIAM HOWE, K B.

ALL INTREPID ABLE-BODIED

HEROES,

WHO are willing to serve His MAJESTY KING GEORGE the Third, in Defence of their Country, Laws and Constitution, against the arbitrary Usurpations of a tyrannical Congress, have now not only an Opportunity of manifesting their Spirit, by assisting in reducing to Obedience their too-long deluded Countrymen, but also of acquiring the polite Accomplishments of a Soldier, by serving only two Years, or during the present Rebellion in America.

Such spirited Fellows, who are willing to engage, will be rewarded at the End of the War, besides their Laurels, with 50 Acres of Land, where every gallant Hero may retire. . . . .

Each Volunteer will receive, as a Bounty, FIVE DOLLARS, besides Arms, Cloathing and Accoutrements, and every other Requisite proper to accommodate a Gentleman Soldier, by applying to Lieutenant Colonel ALLEN, or at Captain KEARNY'S Rendezvous, at PATRICK TONRY'S, three Doors above Market-street, in Second-street.

FAC-SIMILE OF A PROCLAMATION BY SIR WILLIAM HOWE.

BOSTON

ARLES TOWN

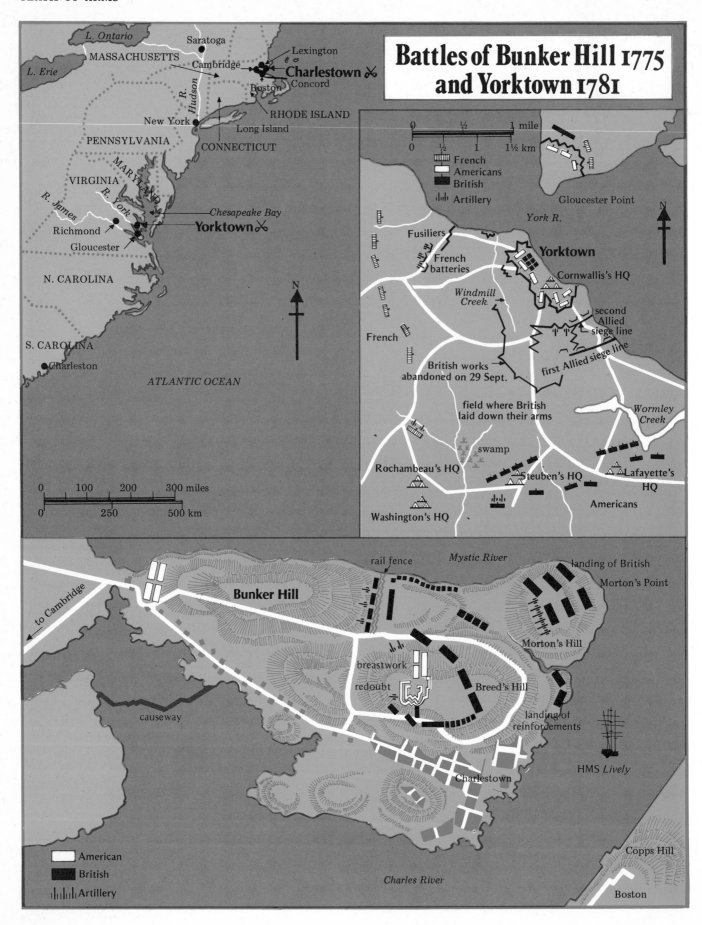

L. Ontario
Saratoga
MASSACHUSETTS
Cambridge
Lexington
Charlestown ✂
L. Erie
Concord
R. Hudson
Boston
New York
RHODE ISLAND
PENNSYLVANIA
CONNECTICUT
Long Island
MARYLAND
VIRGINIA
R. York
R. James
Chesapeake Bay
Yorktown ✂
Richmond
Gloucester
N. CAROLINA
N
S. CAROLINA
Charleston
ATLANTIC OCEAN

0   100   200   300 miles
0   250   500 km

Battles of Bunker Hill 1775 and Yorktown 1781

0   ½   1 mile
0   ½   1   1½ km

🏳 French
☐ Americans
■ British
⑂ Artillery

Gloucester Point
York R.
N

Fusiliers
French batteries
Yorktown
Cornwallis's HQ
Windmill Creek
second Allied siege line
French
first Allied siege line
British works abandoned on 29 Sept.
Wormley Creek
field where British laid down their arms
swamp
Rochambeau's HQ
Steuben's HQ
Lafayette's HQ
Washington's HQ
Americans

rail fence
Mystic River
landing of British
Morton's Point
to Cambridge
Bunker Hill
Morton's Hill
breastwork
redoubt
Breed's Hill
landing of reinforcements
causeway
Charlestown
HMS Lively
☐ American
■ British
⑂ Artillery
Copps Hill
Charles River
Boston

64

ABOVE Lord Cornwallis was commander-in-chief of the British forces at Yorktown. He longed for supplies and reinforcements from New York, but they never came. In the end, he decided to evacuate his army – but, by then, it was too late.

LEFT Back in England, the satirists joyfully sharpened their pencils. This drawing combines a comment on the campaign in North America with a statement on women's hair-styles.

BELOW George Washington was a general who never gave up. He managed to put heart into his army; to hold it together through years of hardship and, occasionally, defeat. Yorktown was the grand climax – the pay-off for Washington's single-minded devotion to his cause.

One of the funny things about the Battle of Bunker Hill was that this feature was one of the few places on the Charlestown peninsula where *no* fighting took place. The rebel militiamen may not have been very accomplished at the art of drill, but they had few peers when it came to digging. Throughout the night of the 16th, about a thousand of them laboured away until, by dawn, they had created an impressive stronghold. Over in Boston, Howe had heard them at work, but he dismissed the sounds as unimportant. They were, he said, merely planning another demonstration; and when, soon after sunrise, HMS *Lively* began to bombard the fat-tongued strip of land, her captain was ordered to desist.

Once the fort had been completed, the rebel commanders studied it with critical eyes. It was well done, but was it *enough*? The flanks were exposed, and so they went to work again, building a stone wall on one side and a breastwork on the other. Putnam, meanwhile, had gone to the nearby town of Cambridge to enlist extra troops. His visit was rewarded by offers of service from General Artemas Ward of the militia and a thousand crack volunteers from the New Hampshire Regiment commanded by Colonel John Stark.

Hand-to-hand fighting during the Battle of Bunker Hill. The British underrated their opponents: they may have looked like a rabble compared with the immaculate redcoats, but their zeal and marksmanship could not be disputed.

On the peninsula, that champion of the rebel cause, Dr Joseph Warren, had arrived carrying a musket. Prescott offered to hand over his command to the physician, but Ward refused. He had, he said, come to fight as an ordinary foot soldier.

Howe landed his force of two and a half thousand troops without opposition; the town of Charlestown was set ablaze by red-hot shot fired by two floating batteries; everything seemed set to teach the rebels a lesson they'd never

forget. The General's plan was to seal off the peninsula by sending his marines into Charlestown; his Light Infantry were to march round by the beach and attack the fort from the rear.

The British general made the fatal mistake of underrating his opponents. They may have looked like a rabble compared with the immaculate redcoats, but nobody could dispute their zeal and their marksmanship. What was more, their commanders had learned the English lesson of holding their fire until the last minute. One of them, Colonel Stark, had driven a stake into the ground forty yards from his position behind the stone wall. Heaven help the militia-man who pressed a trigger before the enemy had passed that point.

Howe's Light Infantry were twice repelled by Prescott's men, who were positioned behind a rail fence covering the shore. The marines were driven out of Charlestown by sharpshooters in buildings that had escaped the flames. And the main body of foot soldiers, burdened with heavy packs, found the going much harder than anyone had expected. No doubt cursing the lack of proper reconnaissance, they were compelled to plod through waist-high grass that concealed rocks and other hazards.

It required three attempts, assisted by reinforcements commanded by Henry Clinton, to occupy the Charlestown peninsula. The operation cost Howe half his force in killed and wounded (rebel casualties amounted to about seven hundred and fifty, but they included Dr Warren); and even then he could not reasonably claim a victory. The American forces were compelled to retreat not because they had been overwhelmed, but because they ran out of ammunition. In a sense, it was they who won the day; in the following year, the British were compelled to evacuate Boston – for ever.

The American Army was born, and George Washington became its first Com-mander-in-Chief. At first it was a raggle-taggle collection of soldiers. Some of the men came from their farms to fight, and many of them went back home at harvest time. Winters were spent in primitive quarters under appalling conditions. Some froze to death; many died from lack of food. But this collection of warriors, garbed in threadbare uniforms, gradually became an efficient fighting force. Washington gave it the will to fight on; an emigrant soldier of fortune from Prussia, named Baron von Steuben, gave it discipline. Washington was the prophet; von Steuben was the drill master. The turning point came in 1777, when a corps of the British army commanded by General Burgoyne was thrashed at Saratoga. In the following year, France came into the war on the side of the Americans. The end had begun . . .

The American War of Independence began on one peninsula; it ended, to all intents and purposes, on another. By 1881, Henry Clinton – now Com-mander-in-Chief – was bottled up in New York, menaced by a Franco-American army commanded by George Washington and Count Donatien Rochambeau. Far from expecting reinforcements from the United Kingdom, General Clinton had been instructed to detach troops to safeguard the West Indies against the French fleet. Down south, Clinton's second-in-command, General Lord Cornwallis, was working his way through the Carolinas, waging – for want of any better orders from New York – a war of his own. Cornwallis's intention was to attack the state of Virginia. According to his way of thinking, it not only made sound strategic sense: by plunging a sword into the heart of Washington's home state, its effect on rebel morale might be catastrophic.

At last Cornwallis received a letter from Clinton. The General was to halt his offensive – at any rate for the time being. Once the threat had been removed from New York, they would think again. For the meanwhile, he was to 'take up a defensive position in any healthy position he preferred'. It gave Cornwallis a good deal of latitude, but it certainly made him aware of the realities of the situation. Whatever assistance he needed, it would be unlikely to come from New York.

For his 'healthy position', Cornwallis chose Yorktown, a place of about sixty homesteads that depended on tobacco for most of its income. It was situated at the head of a neck of land, where the York river poured out into Chesapeake Bay. Since it was protected by water on three sides, and was well placed to receive supply ships from the north, it seemed to be ideal. Unfortunately for the British General, his calculations were based on the assumption that the Royal Navy would retain its command of the sea. In fact, the senior British naval officer, Rear-Admiral Sir Thomas Graves, sailed south with his fleet in an attempt to wipe out the French warships of de Grasse. It should have been a fairly easy battle. Nelson would have sent the enemy scurrying for safety – but Graves was not of Nelson's calibre. He went by the rule book, carrying out laborious drill movements, while the French vessels smashed shell after shell into his warships. Eventually his squadron limped back to New York to refit. Surprisingly, the news of this defeat never reached Cornwallis, though its effects were felt soon enough.

The garrison's food supply was now confined to ship's biscuits and salt beef. Before long, the meat became putrid and the biscuits were infested with weevils. The town's supply of water was infected, and two thousand men went down with dysentery – and the loyalist refugees that poured into the place only added to the havoc. As Cornwallis sadly noted in mid-September 1881, 'the foul fever is spreading, partly on account of the many hardships from which we have had little rest day or night, and partly on account of the awful food.'

When Washington released New York from the threat of attack, it was bad news for Cornwallis. During a march in which his men covered two hundred miles in fifteen days, his troops hurried south to link up with forces on the spot for the investment of Yorktown. An army of 16,645 French and American

The French received news of the British surrender at Yorktown with relish. In this drawing to celebrate the event, de Grasse's naval units were given the prominence they so obviously deserved.

soldiers was now split up into three divisions, laid out in a semicircle against Cornwallis's sick and dispirited 5,300. Their ninety-one pieces of artillery included twenty-four eighteen-inch guns, a number of ten-inch mortars, and a siege train. By 28 September, Washington's men were in position and the barrage began.

Cornwallis still had a chance of escape – if only he would take it. On the far bank of the York river at Gloucester, a detachment of British troops under the command of Colonel Banastre Tarleton was reasonably unmolested. If the General evacuated his men across the river and linked up with Tarleton, he might be able to get away. But Cornwallis was uncertain: he was still looking desperately towards the sea, expecting, or at any rate hoping, that supplies and reinforcements would arrive from New York. But nothing came. Eventually, on 16 October, he gave the necessary orders. But now even the weather conspired against him. When the Light Infantry, the Guards, and part of the 23rd Foot had been embarked, a sudden gale sprang up from seaward. The boats were driven upriver in confusion. The last thread of hope was broken.

Earlier on, the commanding officers of two Guards regiments had made an

The surrender at Yorktown was a terrible humiliation for the British. Cornwallis's troops were compelled to march out of the town, serenaded by the mocking strains of a melody entitled *The World Turned Upside Down*. Washington pointed out that his own men had been treated no less harshly in defeat.

69

attempt to overcome a couple of Washington's redoubts. At the head of three hundred and fifty men, they achieved their objective, spiked eleven guns with their bayonets, and accounted for over a hundred casualties. But without reinforcements they were unable to consolidate their gains, and presently they were driven back with heavy losses.

Yard by yard, the Allies closed in on the stricken garrison. The artillery barrage was heavier than ever and nobody was more zealous in its execution than an American officer named Thomas Nelson. Nelson deserves a special place in the story of the siege of Yorktown. His home was there; and, since it was the best house in the community, he conceived the idea that Cornwallis had probably made it his headquarters. With praiseworthy singlemindedness, he directed his battery of guns to destroy it.

Washington was in a hurry. De Grasse had made it plain that he could not keep French troops and ships in the vicinity for much longer – they had other business to attend to in the West Indies. He need not have worried. On the morning of 17 October, a figure wearing a scarlet jacket climbed over the defences beating a drum. Suddenly the guns were silent: Cornwallis, clearly, wished to discuss the surrender of Yorktown and Gloucester. Presently a note was handed to Washington. 'I propose', wrote Cornwallis, 'a cessation of hostilities for 24 hours, and that two officers may be appointed by each side, to meet at Mr Moore's house, to settle terms . . .' The General, pleading sickness as an excuse, did not attend; his place was taken by a deputy. The date, appropriately, was the anniversary of the Battle of Saratoga.

If the British hoped for lenient treatment, they were to be disappointed. Some while earlier, they had treated the Americans less than generously after the taking of Charleston. Now Washington could make amends. Instead of agreeing that the English troops might return to Britain, the German units to Germany, he insisted that they should go into captivity as prisoners of war. On the morning of the 19th they marched out of the ruins of Yorktown with their colours furled and the band playing (again on Washington's insistence) a horribly apt tune entitled 'The World Turned Upside Down'. Then, in silence, the men grounded their arms. The last major battle in the American war for independence was over.

OPPOSITE Washington and his commanders confer during the siege of Yorktown.

BELOW Troops march towards Yorktown as smoke rises from its bombardment in the distance.

7 The Longest Winter

Borodino 1812

No war-lord in his right mind (the state of Hitler's in 1941 must be regarded as debatable) would willingly attempt the conquest of Russia by land. The distances are so vast, the prospect so bleak, that the country seems to absorb invading armies as if it were an enormous sponge. Napoleon was never unmindful of the joys of conquest, but, shrewd Frenchman that he was, a triumphant clash of arms was not his motive when he set off for Moscow in 1812. He made the journey with reluctance – simply because, as he saw the situation, he *had* to.

The Grand Army's successes in western and central Europe were an economic disaster for Britain. As one nation after another fell to the French forces, the British market for trade crumbled with them. Eventually, all that remained was Russia. In 1810, the Tsar was still buying English goods; what was more, six hundred British merchant ships that had been harried from one end of the Baltic to the other were eventually given sanctuary in a Russian port. Napoleon was right when he called Russia 'the last resort of England'. It was all that stood between the nation and financial ruin.

In an attempt to teach the Tsar a lesson, Napoleon marched his troops into Oldenburg – a place of no particular importance, except that the Grand Duke happened to be the Russian ruler's brother-in-law. The Tsar replied by insisting that all French troops be withdrawn to the west of the River Oder. This was the last straw. A gesture such as the occupation of Oldenburg was obviously not enough. The Russian Emperor would have to be hammered into submission. He was the only flaw in Napoleon's grand design for Europe. Early on the morning of 24 June 1812, Napoleon began his advance into Russia at the head of 680,000 troops. His first objective was the Lithuanian capital of Vilna.

The army had to wait for over two weeks in the town, and this ought to have given Napoleon warning of hazards to come. The reason for the delay was that his supply columns had already broken down. Eventually the situation was remedied, and the gigantic conglomeration of men, horses and artillery pieces moved on. At Vitebsk there was another fortnight's hold-up, this time to give the stragglers a chance to catch up and to establish stores of ammunition. Somewhere out in front there were two Russian armies. One of them, commanded by Barclay de Tolly, amounted to 127,000 men; the other, led by Prince Bagration, had 66,000. Napoleon's plan was to smash through the right wing of Barclay's, thereby preventing the two from coming together. He failed, for the simple reason that after three days of continuous attacks he was still unable to cut the main road to Moscow. On 1 August, the two Russian generals linked up at Smolensk. When some days later Napoleon's army arrived in the town, the place was deserted. The Russian troops had melted away into the great tracts of country that lay between Smolensk and Moscow.

Summer was growing old, and it must have been tempting to go into

Prince Bagration, commander of the Russian second army, was in charge of operations on the left. The prince was able, popular and chivalrous. Watching a French division approaching his positions, he commented, 'Bravo, Messieurs! C'est superbe.' Later, he was mortally wounded.

Napoleon was not at his best at
Borodino. He was suffering from a
heavy cold; his lines of
communication were impossibly
long; and he missed two
opportunities to destroy the
Russians' right flank. The
battle cost him thirty
thousand casualties.

OVERLEAF The Borodino
battlefield. The two great armies
kept pounding away at each other
until both were exhausted.

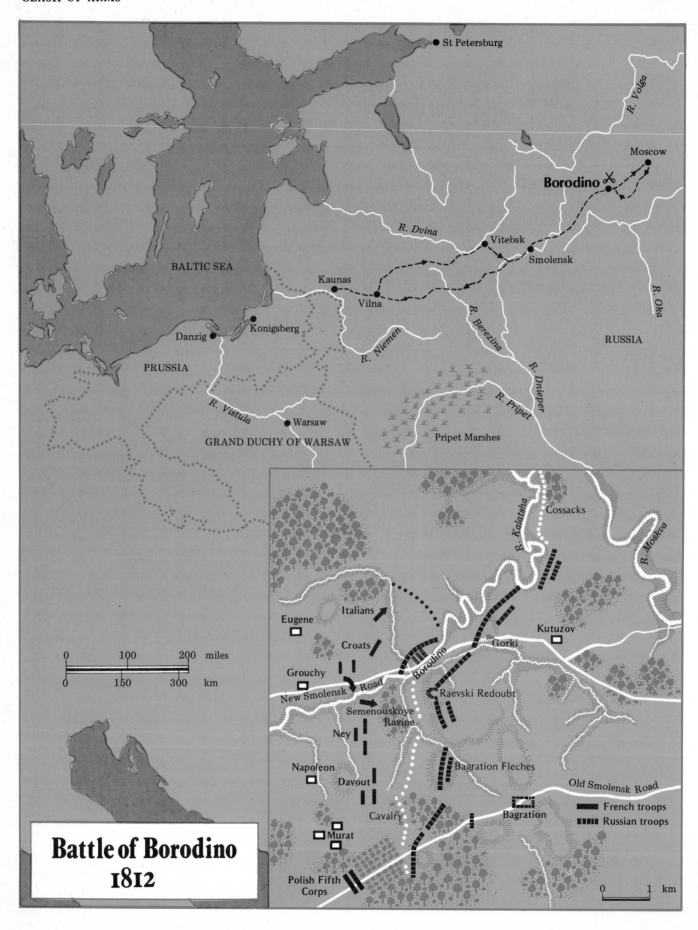

St Petersburg

R. Volga

Moscow

Borodino

R. Dvina

Vitebsk

Smolensk

R. Oka

BALTIC SEA

Kaunas

Vilna

R. Niemen

R. Berezina

R. Dnieper

RUSSIA

Danzig

Konigsberg

R. Pripet

PRUSSIA

R. Vistula

Warsaw

Pripet Marshes

GRAND DUCHY OF WARSAW

0	100	200	miles
0	150	300	km

R. Kalatsha

Cossacks

R. Moskva

Eugene

Italians

Kutuzov

Croats

Gorki

Grouchy

Borodino

New Smolensk Road

Raevski Redoubt

Semenouskoye Ravine

Ney

Bagration Fleches

Napoleon

Old Smolensk Road

Davout

Bagration

Cavalry

French troops

Russian troops

Murat

Polish Fifth Corps

0   1 km

Battle of Borodino 1812

winter quarters and wait for the spring. Three reasons prevented it. The first two were entirely practical: it was impossible to supply the army there, and there was a danger that the link with France might be cut. The other was a delusion that impelled Napoleon to action. Never mind the Russian army – if he could only reach Moscow, the Tsar would capitulate and everything else would be solved. The Grand Army was given its marching orders. Its destination was near the village of Borodino, about a hundred miles from Moscow. It was there that, under the command of an obese seventy-year-old general named Prince Golenischev-Kutuzov, the armies of Barclay and Bagration were encamped; and it was there that Napoleon proposed to smash them. After that, surely, the Tsar would be brought to his knees.

The French army that assembled a few miles from Borodino was not the massive instrument of war that had set out for Russia. Sickness had cut severe holes in its ranks; many of the horses had died, and the survivors were in poor condition. As for Napoleon, he was not at his ebullient best. At one end of his body, a cold made it difficult for him to speak; at the other, a recurring bladder complaint was giving trouble. Significantly, in the battle that was about to take place, his performance was a fair way short of brilliant. He left much of the fighting to his generals; and, when he did interfere, it was usually for the worse.

By this time, the difference in size between the two armies had been substantially narrowed. The French mustered about 130,000, the Russians approximately 120,000. When they were set out in battle order, each occupied a front roughly three miles long, with the infantry forward, the cavalry behind them, and, in the rear, the respective Imperial Guards acting as reserves.

On 5 September, a division of French infantry successfully stormed an

ABOVE LEFT The Russian supremo was Marshal Prince Golenischev-Kutuzov, a man of seventy, who left most of the battle's conduct to his subordinates. Kutuzov was determined to prevent Napoleon from reaching Moscow. But, despite the fact that his army survived Borodino, he failed.

ABOVE Marshal Ney fought with determination and considerable courage. Leading the main attack on the Russians, he scored successes that might have been decisive. But Napoleon did not follow them up. Afterwards, Ney was awarded the title of Prince de la Moskowa.

advanced Russian redoubt in the village of Shevardino. On the following day, Napoleon rode forward to make his reconnaissance. He could see the greater part of the Russian army on the ground in front of him, with Barclay's divisions on the right of the line, Bagration's on the left. In the centre, there was situated a substantial redoubt that had been built by General Raevsky's engineers, and on his extreme right a fortification built on a mound at Utitsa covered the old road to Smolensk.

If Napoleon had listened to one of his corps commanders, an infantry veteran named Davout, he might have fared better at Borodino. Davout's idea was to move up the old Smolensk road, thrust through the surrounding forest, and turn the Russians' left flank. It would surely be better than a head-on clash? Napoleon doubted it. Once again, the enemy would be given a chance to retreat; the battle of annihilation, for which he had worked so long and earnestly, would escape him. No – there would have to be a frontal attack. Only by this strategy could the enemy be compelled to stand and fight.

The night of 6–7 June was foggy. Nevertheless the French units were moved into position, and at five o'clock Marshal Ney reported to his supreme commander that everything was ready. Half an hour later, Napoleon climbed on to his horse and rode to his command post in the recently captured redoubt at Shevardino. The Russian supremo, Kutuzov, had established his head-quarters in Gorki, about a mile to the west of Borodino. At six o'clock, the French guns opened fire on Bagration's redoubts. All told, Napoleon had a hundred of them in this sector of the front, and the barrage should have been sufficiently punishing. Unfortunately, the artillery officers had misjudged the range, and the rounds fell short. They moved forward, closing the distance to thirteen hundred yards. Then they fired again, this time with rather greater success. The Russian guns replied: the battle had begun.

Davout made the first attack on Bagration's redoubts with two infantry divisions. At some point, the Russian general rode out to the front of his line and inspected the oncoming Frenchmen. The sight impressed him. 'Bravo,

OPPOSITE According to a contemporary writer, Prince Eugene de Beauharnais had shown 'since his tender youth that, one day, he would become somebody'. At Borodino, the prince – who was Viceroy of Italy – gave ample evidence of his bravery. What was more, his troops had faith in him

BELOW Napoleon's infantry form a square against a Russian cavalry charge.

ABOVE Tolstoy painted a vivid picture of the events at Borodino in *War and Peace*. Among the illustrations used in a Russian edition, was this impression of a military hospital. With enormous casualties being inflicted on both sides, the surgeons were never short of employment.

ABOVE RIGHT After Borodino, the Russian armies melted into the huge landscape. Napoleon achieved his ambition of occupying Moscow. But, days after his troops arrived in the city, fires broke out. Somewhere in the ashes of demolished buildings the Emperor's dream expired.

Messieurs!' he is said to have exclaimed. 'C'est superbe.' As a spectacle it may have been; as a harbinger of French victory it was less so. The redoubts changed hands several times; Kutuzov moved troops from Barclay's left flank to reinforce Bagration; Napoleon, hearing of a minor success by Ney's corps, relieved the marshal of ten thousand Westphalian soldiers to strengthen Davout's onslaught. The result was that Ney no longer had any reserves.

Borodino was a battle without a clearly defined shape. It was the conflict of two great armies locked in a struggle for hour after hour, gradually wearing each other to pieces. The casualties were atrocious, and they were not confined to mere junior officers and other ranks. Bagration himself was mortally wounded during the morning; two of Davout's divisional commanders were slain; and so it went on. The French tried in vain to turn the left flank of the Russians, but Kutuzov seemed to have endless reserves with which to plug the gaps. And all the time the guns of both sides kept pounding away, until by early afternoon there was so much smoke it was hard to see what was going on.

Over on the left of the French line, Eugene de Beauharnais, the Viceroy of Italy, had taken Borodino. But now he was in serious trouble as three thousand Russian horsemen galloped towards him. His men formed a square (the classic formation for dealing with cavalry). 'Children', said Eugene, 'take your time, take good aim and look the enemy in the eye.' The Russian troopers halted and turned back. Almost immediately, however, five thousand Cossack regulars came at Eugene's men, but they stood firm until, at two o'clock on that blood-drenched afternoon, he was able to order three infantry divisions into the assault. It was preceded by a charge in which the commanding officer was killed, and minutes later his replacement was shot down. But, after two attempts, the infantry was able to move forward.

The Russian left flank was now in shreds; there had been moderate gains in the centre of the line; and Eugene was moving up on the left. But the battle was far from done. Like two tired and battered heavyweights, the armies struggled on. By five o'clock there was still sporadic gun-fire. As for the infantry, there were enormous holes in the ranks. According to one estimate, only a third of those who had originally been committed to battle were still in action. The others were either wounded or dead.

But one unit was still intact – Napoleon's cherished Imperial Guard. These men, the crack soldiers of the Empire, had not fired a shot. Perhaps they were a symbol – but of what? Napoleon had observed that 'when you are 800 leagues from France, you do not wreck your last reserve'. Perhaps not; but when *do* you bring it to battle? This, surely, was decisive enough to warrant such an action. By treating them as the army's sacred cow, the Emperor had given them the status of regimental colours – decorative, meaningful, but for all practical purposes useless.

At last the sun went down. During the night, Kutuzov disengaged and the road to Moscow was clear. It had cost the French 60,000 rounds of artillery ammunition, 1,400,000 cartridges, three divisional generals and 28,000 men. Russian losses were even heavier – 45,000 men. Even so, the Tsar's army had lived to fight another day; and, for Napoleon, the questionable victory at Borodino was the beginning of a most fearful disaster.

On 14 September, the Grand Army with Napoleon at its head marched into Moscow. Nobody knows how it began – it was probably an accident – but for the next five days the city was consumed by fire until only one-quarter of it remained. As if the blaze were a signal, guerrilla forces began to play havoc with the French lines of communication. Nor did the Tsar show any intention of asking for terms. Napoleon had made the fatal mistake of confusing the end with the means. He had been so obsessed with the idea of occupying Moscow that he had overlooked a fundamental fact of life: victory can only be bought by annihilating the enemy's forces. The Russian army was still in the field – injured, perhaps, but certainly not mortally wounded. Why *should* the Tsar have given in?

By 19 October, Napoleon had realized that it was impossible to remain there any longer. Leading 108,000 men and 569 guns into a frosty wilderness, he began the long march home to France. Two weeks later it began to snow. On 28 and 29 November, Kutuzov caught up with him at Beresina and he left a further 25,000 soldiers behind on the battlefield. The Grand Army had virtually ceased to exist: it was now a collection of half-starved troops in danger of freezing to death. On 5 December, the little Emperor, now very much smaller, handed over his supreme command to Marshal Murat, and hurried away to Paris. He reached the city on 18 December. Somewhat inappropriately, he entered it through the Arc de Triomphe.

With Moscow in ruins, his lines of communication in peril, and with winter already well advanced, Napoleon was compelled to retreat. The long journey through the snow cost him an army.

8 Wellington's Triumph, Napoleon's Doom

Waterloo 1815

When Napoleon escaped from his brief exile on Elba and reappeared on the French coast near Cannes, Marshal Ney made a promise to Louis XVIII. He would, he said, meet his former master and bring him to Paris in a cage. It was, perhaps, typical of this quick-tempered, red-haired soldier, and the monarch was foolish if he took the offer seriously. Far from making a captive of the ex-Emperor, Ney embraced him warmly and said how nice it was to see him back. But that was Ney all over: unpredictable – unreliable, some might say.

In fact, it might have been better for Bonaparte if Ney *had* put him into a cage. There would have been no Battle of Waterloo and no subsequent exile to St Helena. Nor, for all their joyous reunion, could their coming together be considered anything but ill-starred. Between them they lost Waterloo – Napoleon because he spent much of the time removed from the fighting, not entirely understanding what was taking place; Ney because, for all his bravery, he often acted in a manner that was only just competent.

Napoleon came home from Elba. In Paris, he busied himself with building an army, which was not a very difficult task. There were many unemployed veterans looking for work, and they were only too glad to re-enlist. As for the armourers, the seemingly endless stream of demands for ordnance kept their factories busy. Far from complaining, they were delighted to watch moribund profits suddenly come to life. By the end of May 1815, the returned Emperor had 284,000 soldiers awaiting his orders. He strung them out along the frontiers of France – concentrating five infantry corps (124,500 men) in the so-called Army of the North, of which he intended to take personal command.

Britain, Prussia and Austria proposed to counter this renewed threat to the balance of power in Europe by marching on Paris simultaneously. If one of them met with a reverse, the others would continue, and a Russian army, led by Barclay de Tolly, would make haste to fill the gap. The Austrian forces were commanded by a marshal named Schwartzenburg, the Prussians by Prince von Blucher, and the British by the Duke of Wellington. In fact, the last of these was a polyglot army. Of its 93,000 men, only 31,000 came from the United Kingdom. The remainder were variously Dutch, Belgians and Germans. By early April, Wellington had established his headquarters in Brussels; on 3 May, he held the first of several discussions with his neighbour to the east, von Blucher.

On 1 June, Napoleon decided to take the initiative. The main threat, he decided, lay to the north. His object must be to attack Wellington's troops before they could establish a link with Blucher's. What he regarded as a certain victory would cause the British government to be overthrown – and replaced, he dared say, by one more favourable to France. After that, he'd

Four examples of French army uniform at the time of Waterloo.

General Gebhard Leberecht von Blucher, Prince of Waklstadt. At Waterloo, the Prussian general was seventy-two years old, and he found the strain considerable. Nevertheless, as he happily wrote to his wife, 'I put an end at once to Buonaparte's dancing'. But, he agreed, 'my friend Wellington' was entitled to some of the credit.

Wellington's march from Quatre Bras to Waterloo.

deal with the Austrians and the Russians. Eleven days later, the Army of the North marched to the Franco-Belgian frontier, where, in an Order of the Day, he told the men: 'The moment has come to conquer or perish.'

Whatever his faults may have been, Napoleon was extremely realistic about matters of security. The first intimation the British and Prussians had of the French army's advance was on the night of 14 June, when Blucher's outposts noticed the flicker of camp fires on the far bank of the River Sambre. By this time, the Army of the North was in possession of Charleroi, and the generals had been given their instructions for the following day. Ney, whose forces were on the left, was to secure the crossroads where the highway between Nivelles and Namur bisected the route to Brussels at Quatre Bras; a second formation, under Marshal de Grouchy, was to attack Prussian units at Ligny; and a third, led by Marshal Erlon, was to act as a mobile reserve, supporting Ney or Grouchy according to whoever needed him most.

The events of the next two days did little credit to any of the more exalted commanders. On the 15th, Ney pushed the Prussians back, but they put up sufficient resistance to enable Blucher to assemble three corps at a point about four miles away. What was more, he did not (as his orders insisted he should) occupy the Quatre Bras crossroads. But nor, come to that, did Wellington – it was left to the Prince of Saxe-Weimar to establish himself at this key point with a small army of eight thousand, most of them either Dutch or Belgians.

Next morning, Wellington rode over to Ligny for talks with Blucher. The Prussian general could, he assured him, count on support from his army – providing it was possible. Then, in the early afternoon, he made his way to Quatre Bras, where the situation had changed dramatically.

Quite early that morning, Ney had decided he ought to do something about taking Quatre Bras. When he saw the Prince of Saxe-Weimar's small army deployed around the crossroads, he decided to move warily. Although he had twenty-two thousand men at hand, he was suspicious. He knew Wellington's tactics from his campaigning days in Spain. It would be typical of the British general to have a much larger force hidden away out of sight. It took him until eleven o'clock to decide that it was reasonably safe to do battle, and another three hours went by before his gunners went into action. When Wellington arrived, the Allied line was beginning to waver.

Anybody interested in miracles should study the engagement at Quatre Bras in detail. At 3.30, just when it was most desperately needed, General Picton's cavalry turned up – followed by a division of Dutch horsemen from the direction of Nivelles, followed by yet another division commanded by the Duke of Brunswick. There was no lack of casualties, but, far from diminishing, the once slender Allied force was growing at an amazing rate. Everyone, it seemed, who had nothing better to do, and who could hear the din of battle, was converging on the crossroads. By five o'clock that afternoon Wellington had thirty thousand troops under his command.

Over in the direction of Ligny, Blucher was having a rough time. Von Bulow, who should have been lending a hand, was too far away to be of any use; Wellington was otherwise engaged at Quatre Bras. The crisis came during late afternoon, when the French went in with the bayonet during a thunderstorm. Shortly afterwards, Blucher's horse was shot from under him, and the seventy-three-year-old marshal was slightly injured. It was left to his chief of staff, General von Gneisenau, to conduct the retreat to a point sixteen miles away to the north. The Prussians had lost sixteen thousand men either killed or wounded, and a further eight thousand had deserted.

OVERLEAF An impression of the Battle of Waterloo by French artist Phillipoteau.

ABOVE In every battle, there is a moment of truth. There may be some time to go before it is resolved; but, from that moment, the result is inevitable. At Waterloo, it occurred when Wellington ordered the general advance. 'No cheering, my lads,' he told his troops, 'but forward and complete your victory.'

While all this was going on, Erlon's corps had been marching to and fro between the two fronts, with nobody making any great demands upon them. On one occasion, the French mistook his men for the enemy, which simply added to a good deal of prevailing confusion.

It was now raining steadily. At nightfall, Wellington decided to withdraw from Quatre Bras. Covered by the Earl of Uxbridge's cavalry, his men made their way back to previously reconnoitred positions on a ridge at Mont Saint Jean, two miles south of a village named Waterloo.

On the right of Wellington's line there was a small chateau, surrounded by an orchard, named Hougoumont. Beyond it, the ground fell away into a valley. In the centre, a farm (La Haye Sainté) stood beside the road from Brussels to Charleroi; and, over on the left, another farm (Papelotte) marked the eastern extremity. Forward of the positions, the ground sloped gently. It had been covered by fields of ripening rye; now the crop had been flattened by the feet of men and horses, the land made soft and muddy by incessant rain. On the Allied side there were 68,000 men and 156 guns, on Napoleon's 72,000 soldiers and 246 guns. In the coming battle, the Emperor was hampered by

OPPOSITE Late on the day of the battle, Wellington and Blucher met at La Belle Alliance. The two generals shook hands without dismounting. Blucher suggested that the inn's name would be a good one for the battle but the Duke preferred Waterloo.

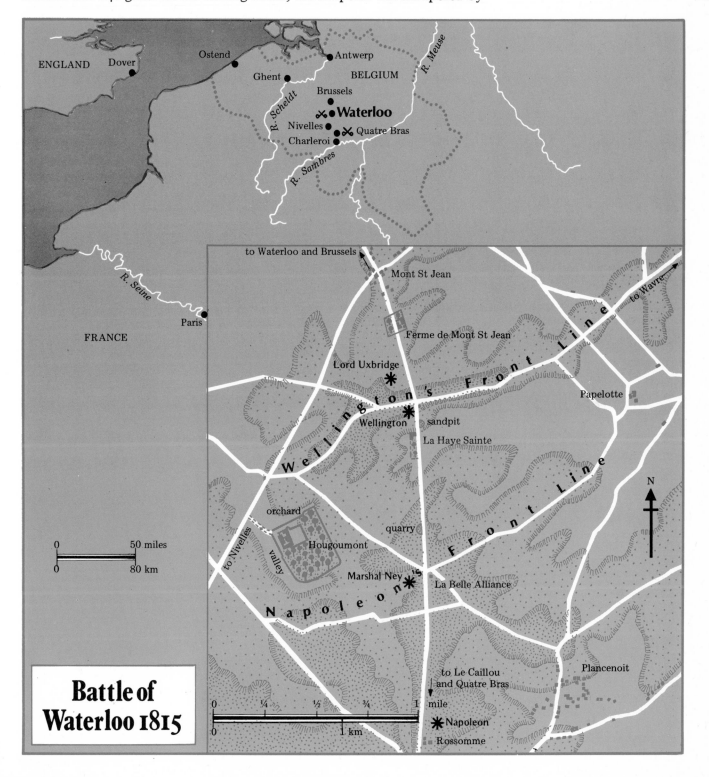

Battle of Waterloo 1815

Napoleon surveys the field as the British line steadily advances along the whole length of the battlefield.

OPPOSITE The battle is over. Forty-seven thousand men have been either killed or wounded. It is a time to dig graves for the dead; to comfort the injured.

what seemed to be a quagmire ahead. It prevented him from bringing his artillery far enough forward.

True to many battles fought by Napoleon, the main attack was to come in the centre of the line. At 11.30 that morning, a force of French infantry made an assault on Hougoumont. It was intended as a diversion – something that would distract Wellington from the area around La Haye Sainté and use up his reserves. As it happened, however, the commanding officer, Jérôme Bonaparte, conceived it on a somewhat grander scale. Consequently he over-stretched himself, and his force suffered heavy casualties from units of the Guards and Dutch and Hanoverian troops. Throughout the day, there was heavy fighting in the area of Hougoumont. Similarly, on the extreme left, the farm at Papelotte changed hands a good many times.

At 1.30 p.m. a bombardment by eighty French guns prepared the way for Napoleon's main assault. After about half an hour, the artillery became silent, and a force of eighteen thousand men, led by Erlon, could be seen struggling up the slope, marching four abreast. Picton came out to meet it with his cavalry. Erlon, who had been wounded late on the previous afternoon at Quatre Bras, was killed almost immediately; the French soldiers faltered. Suddenly, a second formation of British horse, led by the intrepid Lord

Uxbridge, erupted from the Allied line and crashed into the now disorderly
French columns. Three thousand prisoners were taken, but Uxbridge was
discovering that it is sometimes easier to start a cavalry charge than it is to
stop it. There was so much momentum behind his troopers that they plunged
too far towards the enemy lines. When at last the squadrons regained the
ridge, they had suffered heavy casualties.

Napoleon's concept of the battle had been that it would reach a climax with
a massed attack by his cavalry supported by the foot soldiers of the Imperial
Guard. But he was now some way behind the front, and everything was in the
hands of the impetuous Marshal Ney. Ney had been infuriated by the repulse
of Erlon's men; now – in the smoke, the confusion, the excruciating din of
battle – he made a fatal mistake. On the dim horizon ahead of him, he saw
men and wagons making off towards Brussels. In fact these were French
prisoners and Allied wounded, but Ney told himself that they were the
beginning of a general retreat. Now, surely, was the time to strike a final blow.
Without waiting for infantry support, he sent an order back for two regiments
of cavalry. The instructions were misinterpreted. Instead of receiving two
regiments, he was sent eight – twelve thousand horsemen. If the assault failed,
there could be no second attempt. He now had every surviving trooper in the
Army of the North under his command. Possibly he decided that the Emperor
had given these instructions; he may also have assumed that, somewhere in
the smoke to the rear, the infantry were waiting to come up in support. Neither
assumption was true. Napoleon knew nothing about it, and the foot soldiers
were standing by – their lines battered by artillery fire – waiting for something
to happen.

But Ney spent little time considering matters. This was the moment when
France would regain her glory. He gave the order to charge, and the giant
formation of horsemen broke into a canter. As they neared the top of the ridge,
the picture suddenly changed. The departing wagons with their cargoes of
wounded, the straggling prisoners, had vanished. Instead of a retreating
army, Ney found himself confronted by the solid, unmoving squares of
Allied infantry. This, indeed, was the climax of the battle. Again and again
the French horsemen charged. The thunder of guns, the crackle of musket
fire, the clash of steel – the sounds told the story of a battle in which elements
of despair and uncommon courage were evenly mixed. Some of the squares
collapsed; others stood firm. At one point, Ney decided he was winning. He
sent a message back to the Emperor, asking for more troops; the Emperor,
unaccountably, refused. It was not until seven o'clock that foot soldiers of the
Old Guard began to move forward. By then it was too late: the Prussians
under Blucher and von Bulow had arrived; Wellington had been able to shore
up the centre of his line; and events had begun to turn in the Allies' favour.

By late evening, the attacks had been repulsed and only three squares of
the Imperial Guard remained. The rest of the Army of the North was in full
flight, and presently the squares broke up and they too departed. The
casualties added up to fifteen thousand killed and wounded in Wellington's
army, seven thousand in the Prussian, and probably about twenty-five
thousand Frenchmen – plus another eight thousand who were taken prisoner.

The suffering had been atrocious. Lord Uxbridge was one of many who
had a leg amputated. With true patrician calm, he wrote to his wife while
he was being prepared for the operation; while it was taking place, he made
an occasional remark to the surgeon. If his attitude is to be believed, he found
the whole thing mildly amusing. Afterwards, the dismembered limb was

buried by a local farmer. A stone, marking the spot, became a popular tourist attraction. Another officer, whose left arm had been removed, asked for it to be brought back to him. He had forgotten to remove the rings. And, throughout the battle, the Duke of Richmond – his wife had given the legendary ball on the eve of Quatre Bras – could be seen riding from one place to another, accompanied by his sixteen-year-old son and an attendant. Now and then he spoke to a friend or called out encouragement to the troops. The Duke was not taking part, but he was the most courageous of spectators.

Once Napoleon had an idea in his head, it was almost impossible to dislodge it. Even when he was back in Paris, he could not understand why he had been defeated. Whilst admitting that it was 'a frightful disaster', he also said: 'The day was won. The army had performed prodigies; the enemy was beaten at every point; only the English centre still held. Just as all was over, the army was seized with panic. It is inexplicable.' Wellington, a greater realist and a general who believed in centralized control, admitted it had been 'the nearest run thing'. But at least he knew why he won. It was, he said, 'because I was always on the spot – I saw everything, and did everything myself.'

The longest day in Napoleon's life is over. The French forces are in full retreat.

OPPOSITE After the battle – death and silence. Sir Alexander Gordon lies slain on the Duke of Wellington's camp bed – as, a few feet away, the Duke writes his Waterloo dispatch. It had, he observed, been 'the nearest run thing you ever saw in your life'.

9 Blood in the Crimea

Sebastopol 1854–5

When the opposing armies fought in the open, the Crimean War was not without its triumphs for Britain. The Charge of the Light Brigade was an exception – at Alma and Inkerman, for example, the Russians had been defeated. But the siege of Sebastopol was not of this calibre. The soldiers were badly fitted out: they broiled in summer and froze in winter. Until Miss Nightingale arrived, the hospitals were appalling. This was disastrous; for, apart from the normal hazards of battle, there was an unseen killer at work. Its name was cholera, and it probably accounted for more lives than the Russian guns.

Lord Raglan, for most of the time Commander-in-Chief, was one of nature's second-in-commands. In his day he had been an efficient aide to the Duke of Wellington, but as a supremo he was negative. When towards the end of the campaign he died, his place was taken by Lieutenant-General Henry Simpson. General Simpson was not an improvement.

The key to the war was the port of Sebastopol. If the Russians were victorious there, the Anglo-French and Turkish expeditionary force would be driven into the sea. But if Sebastopol was taken, Russia's role as a naval power threatening the Danube and the Mediterranean would be over. To do this, it was necessary to capture two heavily fortified positions, the Malakoff

OPPOSITE As an ancestor of the landing craft that took Allied soldiers ashore on D-Day, this example may be unconvincing. Nevertheless it was used to reasonably good effect at Sebastopol.

BELOW The troops taking part in the Siege of Sebastopol were accommodated in tents. During winter, conditions were extremely cold.

and the Redan. If they fell, the city – naval base and all – would fall into Allied hands, and the conflict would be over.

    As the price for ending a war, the overwhelming of two forts may not seem to be unreasonable. The truth, however, was that it was extremely difficult. A unit of Zouaves in the French army summed up the thoughts of many people, when its men said: 'Sebastopol will fall when there are three Thursdays in a week.' The first attempt was made on 18 June 1855. The date was fixed by General Jacques Pélissier, the French Commander-in-Chief. According to one account, General Pélissier wished it to coincide with the anniversary of Waterloo – though it is hard to see how a Frenchman could regard this as a

ABOVE Lord Raglan, the British commander-in-chief in the Crimea. For many years, he had been an industrious aide to the Duke of Wellington; as a supreme commander, he was less successful. Raglan died during the siege of Sebastopol – though whether from cholera or a broken heart is uncertain.

good omen. Nor, indeed, was it. The adventure accounted for a great many Allied lives in return for nothing.

The prelude began, satisfactorily enough, eleven days earlier, when the French and British guns opened up an intensive bombardment on the two Russian forts. They created fearful casualties (a thousand men a day was one estimate), but this was not sufficient. The Malakoff and the Redan would fall only when infantry went in with the bayonet. The plan was that the French should assault the former, the British the latter.

In the first week in June, General Pélissier's men had thrown themselves at the Malakoff. They almost reached a tower that was the fort's main feature. Then they were driven off by heavy fire. General Raglan's troops simply stood by and watched. On the 18th, both armies were to attack simultaneously. Raglan intended that his army would advance in three columns, each preceded by a detachment of Royal Engineers to remove any obstacles that might be in their way. A force of a hundred foot soldiers was to follow the sappers, then men with bags of wool to place across the barbed wire, and other men with ladders for scaling the ramparts. Finally, a huge force of infantry would move in for the kill. A barrage lasting three hours was supposed to soften up the resistance in readiness for zero hour at six a.m.

Everything went disastrously wrong. Pélissier became alarmed at the casualties Russian guns were carving in the ranks of his men as they stood in the approach trenches. He refused to wait until the gunners had completed their work of destruction. He sent a message to Raglan, saying that he intended to attack at dawn. The British would oblige him by doing likewise. Raglan quickly adjusted his ideas; but the confusion that attended the entire operation was only just beginning. When an eight-gun battery at one end of the line discharged some random shots, the French commanding officers mistook it for the signal to advance. Consequently, they crossed the line ten minutes too early. The effect was to demolish any attempt to synchronize the movements of the two armies. By the time the British began to move, the Russians were ready for them. As they poured along the trenches, the Russian artillery hurled grapeshot at them, and the men fell by the dozen.

After that, there was nothing but death and confusion. A mere hundred men came anywhere near the Redan – but by this time there was only one ladder left. As for the French, the column that should have formed the centre of the force arrived half an hour late. By now they had lost two of their generals, and all along the line a situation that had begun in confusion was now crumbling into total disorder. At seven o'clock, the attack was called off, and the survivors returned to their lines. The French had lost 3,550 men, the British 1,554.

This was Raglan's last offensive. Shortly afterwards he died. The probable cause was cholera – though it may have been from a milder fever accentuated by a broken heart. Certainly, the failure of what should have been the *coup de grâce* had filled him with a most fearful feeling of disappointment, and indeed failure. Nothing, it now seemed to him, had gone right in the campaign. He had been pilloried by the Press – there was no more point in life.

General Simpson took over command of the British forces, and the siege routine was resumed. The week of the three Thursdays was obviously some way off.

By early September, the situation seemed to have reached a complete deadlock. The Allies were entrenched in the plain to the south-west of Sebastopol; the Russians had obviously no intention of coming out to fight.

At first the Russian gun emplacements were nothing more than earth loosely thrown up by shovels. As time went on, however, they became more sophisticated. The embrasures were plastered with moistened clay and faced with strong wicker-work.

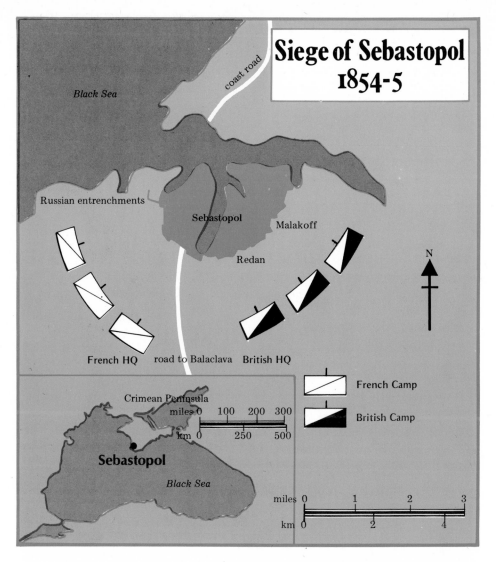

Siege of Sebastopol 1854-5

Black Sea

coast road

Russian entrenchments

Sebastopol

Malakoff

Redan

N

French HQ   road to Balaclava   British HQ

French Camp

British Camp

Crimean Peninsula

miles 0   100   200   300

km 0   250   500

Sebastopol

Black Sea

miles 0   1   2   3

km 0   2   4

The port for operations in the Crimea was Balaclava. By the time this photograph was taken, a small railway had been built to link it with the front line. But the work of landing artillery pieces still depended on human brawn.

Frantic activity by Russian troops inside the Redan during the height of the siege.

OPPOSITE ABOVE Giant mortars, such as these in front of the Light Division, were constantly in action against the Russian fortress. They created substantial casualties; but, as events showed, it took more than artillery to reduce such a strongly defended city.

OPPOSITE BELOW The Siege of Sebastopol. The city had to be taken by the Allies if the threat of Russian naval agression in the Danube and the Mediterranean was to be removed.

The only hope of success lay in another assault on those two dreaded forts, the Malakoff and the Redan.

The morning of 5 September was sunny. A light breeze gently ruffled the grass around the Anglo-French positions. Offshore, the vessels of the fleet rode at their anchors 'as idly [wrote *The Times* war correspondent, William Howard Russell, slightly misquoting Coleridge] as though they were painted ships on a painted ocean'. The Allied guns were blazing away at Sebastopol, but there was nothing remarkable about that. It was so much a part of the daily routine that the troops scarcely noticed it. And then, suddenly, at a point in front of the French positions, an enormous explosion overwhelmed all the other sounds. Three tongues of flame burst out of the ground and seemed to claw at the sky; fragments of earth were hurled a hundred feet into the air. The only thing it could possibly be compared to was the eruption of a volcano.

In fact three mines had been set off by the French. The object was partly to destroy some forward Russian defences, partly to signal the start of a fresh offensive. The artillery barrage intensified; the warships joined in, firing at a range of three miles and pouring shells in the direction of the dockyard. Small arms fire from the French trenches added to the hubbub. This, no doubt about it, was the most punishing bombardment the troops holed up in Sebastopol had ever known. A parapet was blasted to hell; there was 'not one instant', wrote Russell, 'in which the shells did not whistle through the air.' The enemy seemed to be paralysed; as one by one, earthworks were battered into dust, there was no opportunity to repair them. Nothing like it had ever been seen in the history of warfare, and there appeared to be no end to it.

Through the 6th and the 7th, and into the morning of the 8th, the guns maintained their shattering symphony. Each night, it was reckoned, they discharged 150,000 rounds. Nothing, surely, could survive such an ordeal. And, in the vicinity of the Malakoff, not very much did. At noon on the 8th, 36,000 Frenchmen swarmed out of the trenches near the fort and ran across the seven metres that separated them from the enemy. Within two minutes of starting the assault, a soldier was hoisting the tricolour on top of one of the bastions. The Malakoff, that apparently impregnable guardian of Sebastopol, had fallen at last. For the next seven and a half hours, the Russians launched repeated counter-attacks, but Pélissier's men stood firm.

At the same time as the French flag fluttered its message of accomplishment, four rockets were fired. They were the signal for a fresh attack by the British on the Redan. If anybody hoped that Simpson might have benefited

from Raglan's mistakes, he was soon to be disillusioned. Less than fifteen hundred soldiers were earmarked for the assault. One of the first casualties was the brigadier in charge of it. Before long, another brigadier had been wounded, two colonels and one major were dead. The trouble was that, as on the previous occasion, the Russians were expecting them. Indeed, far from being weakened, the garrison at the Redan had been reinforced by survivors from the Malakoff.

The men were now thoroughly demoralized. They were suffering heavy casualties as they moved along the trenches, and there were rumours that the Redan was mined. The Russians *wanted* them to take it: once there were sufficient units established there, they would let off the explosives and blast

The key to Sebastopol was the Redan (seen here) and the Malakoff. If these forts could be taken, it was assumed that the rest of the city would fall.

them all into eternity. Far from leaping eagerly into the fray, the soldiers paused. This was suicide, and they were not ready to die.

As if to make matters worse, the regiments now became mixed up. Officers were wandering up and down the chaotic lines, looking for their men. Soldiers in the 19th Foot refused to take orders from their superiors in the 88th; men in the 23rd declined to obey *anyone* from another unit. Reinforcements were arriving in a dribble, but they served only to create more confusion by squeezing the already overcrowded trenches beyond their capacity. Colonel Sir Charles Windham, who was now in charge, decided that the only hope lay in support from Sir William Codrington's Light Division. After a succession of messengers had failed to reach Sir William, the Colonel came to the conclusion that the only way in which to produce results was to go to Codrington himself. There was now, to all intents and purposes, nobody in command up front.

The mission was not a success. Sir William hesitated, clearly reluctant to commit his precious cavalry. Windham tried to reassure him; but, by the time they had finished arguing, both men noticed that their very unvictorious army was turning tail. What was more, the Russians were pursuing them with rifles and bayonets, and in some cases hurling stones at them. A burst or two of artillery fire put a stop to this, but, one hour after it had begun, the affair was over. The price of ineptitude could be seen in the dreadful piles of dead and wounded that now littered the forward trenches.

Pélissier was not impressed. General Simpson, he assumed, would make another attempt. Simpson replied that he didn't feel in a condition to do so. Whether the General was speaking of his own state of mind, or that of his army, is uncertain. It would have been possible: the Guards, the Highlanders,

the 3rd and 4th Divisions, and most of the reserves, had not yet been committed. Since these units contained some of the army's crack troops, they might have been successful. But the casualties would have been appalling.

Eventually, Simpson decided that he would resume the offensive at five o'clock on the following morning. Or he thought he might. At three o'clock, his officers were still uncertain of his intentions. But by then they did not matter very much. Some hours previously, a loud explosion from Sebastopol made it plain that the Russians had blown up one of the city's main fortresses. At midnight, there was a strange silence the like of which had never been heard before. Other explosions followed, and presently the outer defences became silhouetted against a backdrop of fire. The enemy, obviously, was pulling out. The Redan was unimportant: it had been enough to take the Malakoff. At dawn French troops moved cautiously into the city. By five o'clock some of them were returning with plunder. The Crimean War was as good as over.

The life of Sebastopol as the Tsar's naval base on the Black Sea came to an end early on the morning of 9 September 1855. By 4 a.m., the whole town seemed to be on fire; and, now and again, there was a tremendous explosion. When the sun came up, the last of the defenders could be seen making a hurried exit over a bridge. The Crimean War was, to all intents and purposes, over.

10 The Battle that Forged a Nation

Gettysburg 1863

Gettysburg was, perhaps, the most spectacular battle of the American Civil War. It was also a turning point. It put a full stop to General Robert E. Lee's dream of invading the Northern States. Since this was essential for a Confederate victory, it marked the beginning of the end for Lee. And yet, strangely enough, it happened almost by accident. Indeed, its very location was a place of no particular importance.

Lee's soldiers were in high spirits. They had inflicted a very reasonable score of defeats on Major-General Joe Hooker's Federal Army; now they were driving into Pennsylvania. Once across the Potomac River, the way appeared to be open to such places as Baltimore, Philadelphia and Washington itself. Somewhere, moving in the same direction on a parallel course, there was Hooker's force of about ninety thousand troops. But, after the river crossing, the Confederate cavalry lost touch. Since neither side was anxious to commit itself to a major battle, it did not seem to matter very much.

On 28 June 1863, Lee received two vital pieces of intelligence. One was that the Unionists were concentrating in the town of Frederick, about fifteen miles away on their eastern flank. The other was that Lincoln had lost patience with Hooker. The General had been replaced by George Meade. Joe Hooker, despite his undoubted courage, had few of the qualities required of a commander-in-chief. Meade was a very different matter. He was tough, quick-tempered and, above all things, decisive.

Meade quickly decided that the best place from which to block the way north was at Pipe Creek, about half-way between Frederick and the small

OPPOSITE The Confederate commander-in-chief, Robert E. Lee, on his horse, Traveller.

RIGHT Army encampment on the edge of Gettysburg.

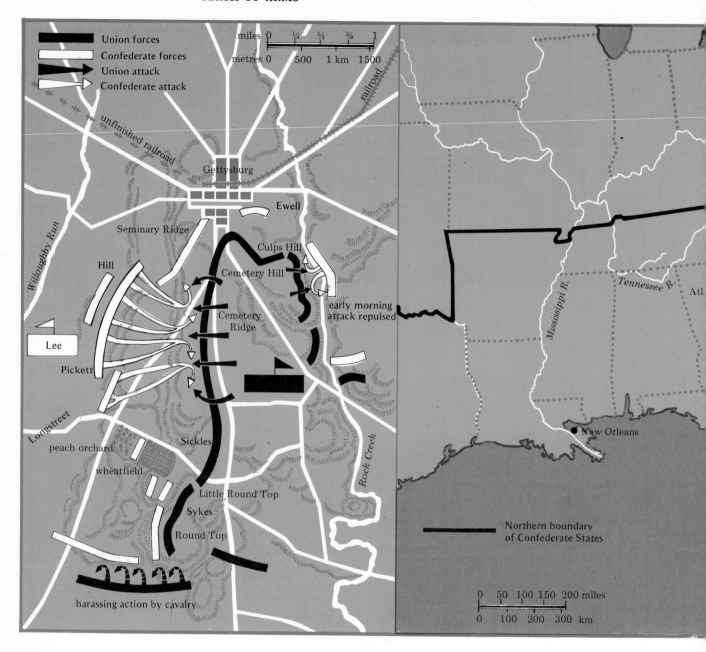

▬▬▬	Union forces
▭▭▭	Confederate forces
◼▶	Union attack
▭▷	Confederate attack

miles 0 ¼ ½ ¾ 1
metres 0 500 1 km 1500

railroad

unfinished railroad

Gettysburg

Ewell

Seminary Ridge

Culps Hill

Hill

Cemetery Hill

Cemetery Ridge

early morning attack repulsed

Lee

Pickett

Willoughby Run

Longstreet

peach orchard

Sickles

wheatfield

Rock Creek

Little Round Top

Sykes

Round Top

harassing action by cavalry

Mississippi R.

Tennessee R.

Atl

New Orleans

▬▬▬ Northern boundary
of Confederate States

0 50 100 150 200 miles
0 100 200 300 km

town of Gettysburg. He took up a defensive position and waited. He was still uncertain where, precisely, the Confederate forces were – just as they were unaware of his location. This gap in his knowledge had to be rectified. He sent off a division of cavalry, commanded by Major-General John Buford, in what he assumed might be the direction of Lee's advance. To support them, in case they encountered the enemy, he dispatched Major-General John Reynolds with three corps of infantry – about a third of his army.

On 1 July, the horsemen dismounted and occupied a ridge to the north-west of Gettysburg. As it happened, the Confederate III Corps was marching towards the very same ridge. It was purely a matter of chance. Lee had been unable to maintain his supply lines and his army was now living off the country. Somewhere out in front, there was said to be a store containing rich quantities of footwear. Lieutenant-General A. P. Hill, the commanding officer of III Corps, had been ordered to appropriate them.

When Buford informed Meade that he had made contact with what might

PREVIOUS PAGES Many artists afterwards depicted scenes of the fighting. They combined realism with heroics. The smoke and blood were all too real – and the heroics abounded.

New York

Gettysburg

Potomac R.

Baltimore

Washington

ttle of Gettysburg 1863

be the Confederate advance guard, the latter was not particularly impressed. He still believed that the battle, if there were to be one, would take place at Pipe Creek. Nevertheless Reynolds was instructed to hurry: it might well be that Buford's dismounted horsemen would need his support.

The Battle of Gettysburg, for this was the beginning of it, lasted for two and a half days. It began on 1 July, brought about by this accidental encounter; it ended during the morning of 3 July. For the first two days, events seemed to be going in favour of the Confederates, but it would have been wrong to draw any conclusions from this. For one thing, Lee was fighting only a portion of Meade's army – the remainder had to be brought up from Pipe Creek, about fifteen miles away. For another, the Unionists might have been better served if one of their generals, Sickles, had not decided to re-write his orders.

By 2 July, Meade's intentions had become clear. Everyone, whether he liked it or not, was being drawn towards Gettysburg. It was here, and not at Pipe Creek, that the battle would be fought. The ground might not be of Meade's own chosing, but he would have to do the best he could. Piece by piece, in the face of increasingly tough Confederate opposition, he laid out his line of defence. It was situated on the high ground to the south of Gettysburg, and the shape was rather like the mirror image of a question mark. Perhaps it was appropriate; for, until the final showdown, the outcome of Gettysburg was one of the war's biggest question marks.

At the north-eastern end of the line, there was a knob of ground known as Culp's Hill; to the west of it (and due south of the town), Cemetery Hill, after which the line stretched southwards for about a mile atop Cemetery Ridge. Finally it ended in two more hills, Little Round Top and Round Top. To the west of Cemetery Ridge there was a valley. On the far side of it, the ground rose again to form Seminary Ridge.

Dan Sickles had been instructed to occupy Little Round Top and Round Top with the Unionist III Corps. Had he done so, his position would have been very hard to take. Instead, doubtless thinking he knew best, he skirted round to the north-west of the high ground, stringing out his troops in a peach orchard and a wheatfield in the valley. It was, as General Sickles was soon to realize, a grave mistake.

The first day's fighting was largely a matter of jockeying for position, of comparatively easy successes for the Confederates, and desperate attempts by Reynolds to contain the situation until the rest of the army arrived. During the late morning the Federal general was killed. To replace him, Meade sent up the commander of his II Corps, Winfield S. Hancock. Not only had Hancock to take over the troops, he had also to send word back about the suitability of the Gettysburg area as a battlefield. He reported favourably.

But there would be no victory that day, or on the following. Things were going very well indeed for the Confederates. The fact that Lee's men had found the going so relatively easy on 1 July, was largely due to the fact that there were some thirty thousand of them on the field – whilst only twenty thousand Unionists had arrived. Similarly, they had ninety guns against only sixty belonging to the opposition. Late in the afternoon, Lee ordered Richard Ewell, the officer in charge of II Corps, to attack Cemetery Hill 'if possible'. It might have been a decisive stroke, but Ewell decided it was *not* possible. His men were too tired. Nothing could be done until he was joined by his third division. The division arrived one hour before sunset, but Ewell continued to do nothing. For the time being, at any rate, the northern end of the Union line was secure.

On 2 July, Lee devoted himself to trying to smash the Federal flanks. Sickles was driven out of his tenuous positions in the orchard and wheatfield. He paid for his misguided initiative with heavy casualties among his troops and with one of his own legs (it was shattered by a cannon ball). Eventually the situation was redeemed by Major-General George Sykes, who took over Round Top and Little Round Top with Meade's v Corps. Lee had instructed Lieutenant-General James Longstreet to launch a lethal thrust at the Unionist left flank (now in shreds after Sickles's thrashing) with his I Corps, but Longstreet seemed to display a lack of interest. Afterwards, he denied having received the order, which seems unlikely. Why, then, did he hesitate? According to some accounts, he was sulking. His idea had been to avoid a clash with the Federal troops at Gettysburg, to thrust on towards Washington. Lee had chosen to ignore his advice, and Longstreet was displeased.

This was undeniably true; but a more likely reason for the General's apparent disregard of orders was the fact that, to get them into position for an attack, he had to move twelve thousand soldiers through difficult and thickly-wooded country. It may have been a good idea; but, in Longstreet's opinion, it was not yet a practical proposition.

When the sun went down on a sweltering 2 July, Ewell had smashed into Federal positions at Culp's Hill; the position on Cemetery Hill was threatened; and Cemetery Ridge was in jeopardy. The Confederates were in possession of Gettysburg itself, though this did not amount to very much, for the town was of small importance. Late that night, Meade held a council of war in a farmhouse on the reverse side of Cemetery Ridge. The fighting so far had cost him twenty thousand men – though he suspected Lee's losses were greater. Did his generals believe, as he did, that they should stand firm? Or would it be more prudent to withdraw? The meeting was unanimous: fight on. The Confederates had spent the previous day battering at his flanks. In the morning, if Meade was any judge, they would attack the centre of the line. Having failed to overwhelm the ends of it, they had (Meade explained) only the centre left.

He was right. The Confederates were massing in the woods on Seminary Ridge. On the following morning, they opened up with 140 guns on the Cemetery Ridge positions. After the initial exchange of shots, the Federal chief of artillery decided to cut down his rate of fire. It would, he reasoned, be better to conserve his ammunition until the enemy was within point-blank range. With this in mind, he removed some of his cannon to the rear of the ridge.

The action was noticed by the chief Confederate gunner, who assumed that the enemy was pulling back. Now, surely, was the time to attack – especially as his supplies of ammunition were running low. He passed the information on to Major-General George Pickett, commander of a division, who went off to consult General Longstreet. What should he do? Pickett wanted to know. Assault Cemetery Ridge? Longstreet simply shrugged his shoulders. The unfortunate Major-General would have to make up his own mind.

As far as Pickett could see, there was no option. There was no point in waiting until the artillery had run out of ammunition, so he assembled his fifteen thousand soldiers on Seminary Ridge and ordered them to advance.

In the centre of the Union line, on top of the ridge opposite, there was a clump of trees. This was the target. Reach the trees, and the enemy would be cut in two. The attack was spearheaded by a brigadier-general named Louis Armistead, who was wearing a slouch hat. They reached the Federal line,

OPPOSITE ABOVE The ultimate weapon. The range of this Federal artillery piece was said to be nearly two miles – and, its manufacturers claimed, it was accurate.

OPPOSITE BELOW Lieutenant-General Longstreet's troops attack at the peach orchard.

OVERLEAF The Confederate assault ran out of thrust as the men stormed strong Federal positions on the all too appropriately named Cemetery Ridge. This was the decisive moment in the battle.

General Gordon Meade, commander of the Federal forces. He was a reliable, professional soldier, a man who always remained calm in a crisis.

OPPOSITE ABOVE The Prisoners. Captured Confederate soldiers are examined disdainfully by a Unionist officer.

OPPOSITE BELOW The losers. One regiment lost eighty per cent of its men; casualties on both sides amounted to nearly forty-six thousand.

overran a battery, and about two hundred and fifty men broke through. But the success lasted for a matter of seconds. Armistead was shot almost immediately, and the rest of the two hundred and fifty were either killed or taken prisoner.

The rest of Pickett's formation now marched into the face of murderous fire. When he was five hundred yards from the clump of trees, he halted and changed direction slightly. This was a mistake. Two brigades were now isolated on the right. Bravely – foolishly, perhaps – Pickett and his men plodded on up the slope. In front of them was a stone wall with some fence rails slung on top of it. As they climbed over them, they found themselves faced by the rifles of Hancock's 11 Corps. Firing at point-blank range, it was impossible for the Federal soldiers to miss. The line wavered, and then disintegrated. One moment there had been an orderly formation of Confederate troops hurrying towards that all-important clump of trees; the next there was only death and flight. Whatever might be happening elsewhere, the cream of Lee's army had spent itself on the all too aptly named Cemetery Ridge.

Lee's only possible course now lay southwards. The army scarcely stood upon the order of its going, but went at once. Gettysburg had cost them dear; but Meade had lost no fewer than twenty-three thousand men. He was in no position to follow up his victory, and the Confederates escaped his wrath. But from then onwards the gates to the Northern States were closed. As Abraham Lincoln said when he dedicated the National Cemetery at Gettysburg, a great many young Yankees had given their lives 'that [the] nation might live'. Yes – and a great many Confederates as well.

II Chaos on the Road to Ladysmith

Spion Kop 1900

Among the earlier events of the Boer War, at least two favoured the Dutch settlers. One was the investment of Ladysmith, a town in Natal, where a British force of twelve thousand troops was kept away from action for the next four months. The other was the choice of a British Commander-in-Chief. His name was Sir Redvers Buller.

Sir Redvers was sixty when the war broke out on 10 October 1899. He was a brave man – no doubt about that. In the Kaffir War of 1877, he had been awarded the Victoria Cross. The soldiers liked him, which was to his advantage; but popularity and courage are not enough. Say what you may, Sir Redvers was not one of the great military brains of his own or any other time.

In his first attempt to relieve Ladysmith, Buller was defeated at Colenso. There was nothing wrong with his army: the General had shown his inadequacy by piling one mistake on top of another. His judgment, never very acute, had been marred still more by a near miss by a Boer shell. Superficially, his injuries amounted to no more than some bruised ribs. In fact, General Buller had been shell shocked.

The Government in London had been less than impressed by Buller's performance. Field-Marshal Lord Roberts was instructed to pack his belongings and proceed to Cape Town. He, perhaps, would do better. While Roberts was on the high seas, Buller would have to do the best he could. His force had been strengthened by the arrival of a new division, which brought the total to more than thirty thousand men.

Welcome as the reinforcements undoubtedly were, their commander, Lieutenant-General Sir Charles Warren, did little to improve Buller's spirits. Warren's military career had been adequate, if far from spectacular. At one point it had been interrupted by a spell of two years as Chief Commissioner of the Metropolitan Police. More recently he had retired. He was a man with a passable intellect and a vile temper. His experience of handling large bodies of troops was somewhat limited (as a Royal Engineer by background, he had only the most vague idea of how to employ cavalry), and he was a prey to that most dangerous of maladies in the mind of a high commander – obsessions. Once a notion fixed itself in the head of Sir Charles, it was impossible to dislodge it. Nevertheless, when he had sailed for the Cape in the *Norham Castle*, he carried with him a commission of extreme importance. If, for any reason, Buller was unable to carry out his duties, he was to take over as Commander-in-Chief until the arrival of Roberts.

Sir Redvers Buller and Sir Charles Warren disliked each other on sight. The former did his best to make the latter uncomfortable – he was even heard to refer to Sir Charles as 'that dug-out ex-policeman'. On the credit side, however, was the fact that they now had one of the most potent armies that had ever been assembled. It amounted to 24,000 infantry, 2,600 cavalry, eight

General Sir Redvers Buller. Like Roberts, he had won the Victoria Cross as a more junior officer. His conduct of the campaign in South Africa, however, was catastrophic.

field batteries, ten naval guns, and an enormous waggon train carrying supplies. The Boers were nothing if not resourceful; they travelled light, and were therefore extremely mobile. Initiative was a quality that, in the British soldier, was apt to be discouraged. So long as he fought bravely, and died without complaint, little more was asked of him. The business of maintaining him in the field required a huge assembly of transport, which rendered the force cumbersome and inflexible. It was a feature of campaigning that figured high on Sir Charles Warren's list of obsessions. All would be well, he told himself many times, if the supply column was present and correct.

The road to Ladysmith was barred by a range of tall hills on the far side of the Tugela river. Among them was a small mountain, 1,470 feet high, named Spion Kop. Whoever held it, or so it seemed, would command all the surrounding countryside. Capture it, and the way to the beleaguered garrison would be clear.

One might have imagined, then, that there were many good reasons for attacking Spion Kop. Buller's motive, however, was less sensible: he wished to rid himself of Warren. He had, perhaps, more than enough reason to complain. He had given Warren the task of piercing the barrier of which Spion

OVERLEAF The rugged terrain which was an added difficulty in the British army's conflict with the Boers is shown in this picture of a Boer's farm.

Kop was a part. Sir Charles had made his way ponderously to the western edge of the range, misusing his cavalry, continually fretting about the waggon train, and fighting small engagements of no importance – apparently with the idea of giving his troops battle experience. Instead of the lightning thrust, the decisive penetration, Sir Charles had dallied. Not unreasonably, Sir Redvers had lost patience. As if on a whim, he issued his colleague with the order: either attack Spion Kop, or else retreat back across the river. It would, he rather hoped, compel Warren to resign (though it is not easy to see why).

Predictably, Warren did not resign. He applied himself to selecting a brigade for the assignment. His first choice of a commander was Brigadier-General Talbot Coke, who had arrived that very same day to take over 10 Brigade. Since Coke was recovering from a broken leg, he may not have appeared the ideal officer to attempt the capture of a mountain. However, Warren was reminded that, on board the *Norham Castle*, he had promised another general, E. R. P. Woodgate, the first taste of blood. Coke stood down and Woodgate took over.

At 7.30 p.m. on Tuesday, 23 January 1900, 1,700 officers and men assembled for the assault on Spion Kop. Each had been issued with a hundred and fifty rounds of ammunition. Since, however, the bayonet and the rifle butt were the intended weapons for the coming fray, and nobody wanted a gun to be discharged accidentally on what was obviously going to be a difficult ascent to

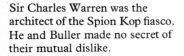

Sir Charles Warren was the architect of the Spion Kop fiasco. He and Buller made no secret of their mutual dislike.

the summit, the troops were forbidden to load their magazines. Two Kaffirs had been impressed to act as guides. One of them bolted soon after the expedition set off; the other was useless. Fortunately, Lieutenant-Colonel A. W. Thorneycroft had spent most of the previous day studying the route through his glasses. Although he was a giant of a man, weighing twenty stone, Colonel Thorneycroft turned out to be surprisingly agile. Leading a forward troop of his Mounted Infantry regiment, he conducted the column to the top without any misadventures. The only living creature the brigade encountered was a large white dog that came to meet them. It was entrusted to a bugler, who made an extempore leash from his rifle pull-through.

Nor was the opposition on the summit of any great moment. It amounted only to a detachment of Boers, who were promptly dispatched after a brief bout of hand-to-hand fighting. It was not surprising. Spion Kop was an ideal observation post, but that was all. The idea of establishing a sizeable force on a mountain top was preposterous.

Once the summit had been reached, all manner of snags became apparent. The ground was too rocky to permit the engineers to prepare adequate trenches. Short of running up and down the mountain, the only way of transmitting signals was by heliograph, a device that works by reflecting the sun's rays. When the sky is overcast, it cannot function. At first light they discovered that they were occupying the wrong part of the summit, that in

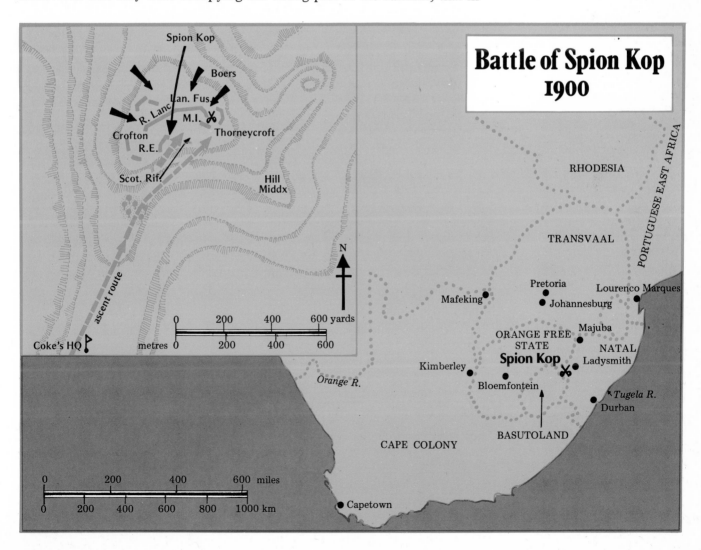

front of them there was dead ground over which the enemy could attack unmolested. Consequently they had to move to new positions. Nor had they enough water, enough medical supplies, or enough surgeons.

Such deficiencies did not seem to argue well for the day that lay ahead. Down below at his headquarters, Warren was doing little to help the situation. His guns could not give supporting fire, nor did it occur to the General that a diversionary attack on some other feature might be a good idea. At least it might have upset the enemy's plans to recapture the mountain. As things were, the small army was crammed together on this table in the sky, waiting without assistance for the Boer vengeance.

It came – shortly after sunrise. During the early reconnaissance, it had seemed that the only way up Spion Kop was from the south. The enemy quickly demonstrated that there were other perfectly good routes. But the most deadly reply came from the Boer artillery. Throughout the long day they plastered the summit with guns and pompoms. Men died and men lay wounded: there was no shelter from this dreadful barrage, and no way of evacuating the injured. Soldiers were crying out for water; but there was none left. Nor were there enough bandages to stem the flow of blood.

Brigadier-General Woodgate was one of the early casualties. Warren appointed an officer named Crofton to succeed him. But Buller, who – although he had delegated responsibility to Warren – couldn't resist any opportunity to interfere, overruled him. This, he announced, was not an action in which Crofton was likely to excel. Thorneycroft, despite his juniority, should take charge. Unfortunately, nobody bothered to inform Crofton. When, later, he was wounded, Lieutenant-Colonel A. W. Hill had arrived with reinforcements from the Middlesex Regiment. Since Hill was now the senior officer, he assumed that he was in command. But this time Thorneycroft was not told. Indeed for much of the afternoon there were two officers running the battle, without either being aware of the other.

The top of Spion Kop had become like a corner of hell transported into the sky. Brigadier-General Lyttelton, who had an independent command

BELOW LEFT The Boers always travelled light and their nightly camps were of the simplest kind.

RIGHT The British entrenchment on the summit of Spion Kop was made with difficulty as the ground was very rocky.

BELOW Boers attacking British infantry on a hill.

a few miles to the east, decided to capture another hill in a most praiseworthy attempt to ease the agony. Buller heard about it, flew into a rage, and ordered it to be cancelled. He spoke too late: the force was already on its way. The height was taken; Buller's rage reached bursting point; and the troops had to be withdrawn.

It was Thorneycroft who, when the sun went down, decided that this macabre farce could not continue. He gave the order to evacuate the mountain top; the troops – including Colonel Hill – followed him. Ironically, the Boers had now reached the conclusion that Spion Kop could not be retaken. They, too, were pulling out. But, since the Earl of Dundonald's horsemen were busy guarding Warren's precious baggage train, when they might have been scouting around, nobody knew about this.

When Buller heard that Spion Kop had been abandoned, he observed that it was understandable. The whole project was a bad idea; they would go to Ladysmith by another route. The besieged garrison was eventually relieved on 28 February. All the cavalry horses had by now been eaten and the evening meal was reduced to a cup of tea. When the inhabitants heard that Dundonald's horsemen were at the gates, they went on drinking their tea. There had been too many false hopes.

As for the Boers, the battle of Spion Kop served to strengthen their idea about the British high command. It had once been a joke amongst them that the killing of an English general was an offence punishable by death. Now they were more inclined to take the notion seriously. Perhaps the ineptitude of such men as Buller and Warren was, after all, their best ally. The final item in the list of follies that attended the Battle of Spion Kop had occurred shortly after nightfall. Warren had wanted to send a message to the mountain top. It turned out to be impossible: the signalling lamps had run out of oil. Such oversights as this could not fail to impress the enemy.

ABOVE Not very long ago, he was a farmer. Now he is a Boer commando – wounded in the slaughter that has disfigured a mountain top. He is taken away to a first aid post, while his comrades keep the battle going.

LEFT A lonely hilltop in South Africa suddenly became the scene of bitter fighting. When it was all over, the cost was many lives – in return for nothing. The living departed; the dead were buried in mass graves.

12 The Tanks are Coming

Cambrai 1917

Calculated in terms of carnage, the first day of the Battle of Cambrai – which set ablaze a small corner of the Western Front in 1917 – was quite a modest affair. Nevertheless, it, more than any other affray in the First World War, marked a turning point. For the first time on the scene of human conflict, tanks were used on a large scale. Not since Hannibal had employed elephants against the Romans had such an unorthodox weapon been seen.

The irony of it is that, from the very beginning of the war, the British high command had possessed the means of employing tanks. Had more people been vouchsafed the sense to develop and use them, the struggle might have been over very much earlier. It would certainly not have produced the casualties that static warfare incurred for a few yards of mud gained or given.

Surprisingly enough, the credit for the introduction of armoured fighting vehicles belongs to the Royal Navy. As early as 1902, a pioneer of the automobile industry named Frederick Simms designed an armoured car on which a machine gun was mounted. He offered his idea to the War Office and it was turned down. Twelve years later, however, when the Royal Naval Air Service took over a number of airfields in Belgium and Northern France, the First Lord of the Admiralty, Winston Churchill, was more perceptive: armoured cars seemed to be the logical way of defending them, and he placed an order.

Churchill was intrigued. If a vehicle could be used to safeguard the security of aerodromes, might it not have a wider application? The First Lord's imagination went to work on the idea, and presently a word was coined: *landships*. They would be large, heavily-armoured and heavily-armed contraptions that could traverse the countryside in much the manner of a ship crossing the sea. On Churchill's insistence, a so-called Landship Committee was set up to investigate the project.

In Flanders, the German thrust spent itself after the Battle of Ypres, and a stalemate took possession of the opposing armies. The Germans tried to break it by the use of poison gas; both sides produced heavier artillery concentrations; but the situation remained immovable.

Meanwhile, unknown to the Admiralty, an army officer named Lieutenant-Colonel E. D. Swinton was pursuing his own line of investigation. The Landship Committee had been working on the theory that the secret of producing cross-country performance was to equip the vehicles with exceptionally large wheels. It was fraught with snags, and the Admiralty should have known better. When steam engines were introduced to ships, they had vigorously opposed the use of paddle-wheels, for the very good reason that these were too vulnerable. The same logic applied to landships.

Colonel Swinton, on the other hand, was much nearer the mark. He calculated that, if armoured cars were fitted with caterpillar tracks, they would be able to crush barbed wire and cross over trenches. The War Office was not impressed. When Churchill heard about the idea, however, he took

BELOW A tank belonging to F Battalion grapples with the enemy's barbed wire. The crew of a steel monster such as this was eight men – plus three carrier pigeons to convey messages.

OPPOSITE A First World War poster depicts the enemy as an inhuman being.

British tanks had first been in action on a small sector of the front during the Battle of the Somme. In preparation for the Battle of Cambrai, they carried out training exercises in a wood behind the lines.

One of the advantages of a tank was that it could cross trenches. That, at any rate, was the theory. Some failed to accomplish it – as, for example, 'Hyacinth' of the Tank Corps's H Battalion which fought in the centre of the British line.

it up with the Prime Minister, Herbert Asquith. Mr Asquith did nothing.

But Swinton was a determined man. His faith could not be shaken by a few refusals. He continued working on the idea, and talking about it, until at last Sir John French, Commander-in-Chief of the British Expeditionary Force, became interested. It was now 1915. Later that year, General Sir Douglas Haig took over, and he, too, murmured cautious encouragement.

Inevitably, a union between the Landship Committee and the Army had to come about. The fusion took place in the summer of 1915. Swinton's specifications were accepted as a starting point; and, after a while, two prototypes were prepared for trials. One was known as 'Little Willie', the other as 'Big Willie'. The former was virtually an armour-plated box mounted on caterpillar tracks. King George V came to watch its performance one day in September 1915. It was, perhaps, disappointing. Its balance was uncertain, and it turned out to be incapable of crossing the width of a trench.

'Big Willie' was much more successful. It was powered by a hundred and five horsepower six-cylinder sleeve valve engine that pushed it along at three and a half miles per hour. It weighed twenty-eight tons, was twenty-six and

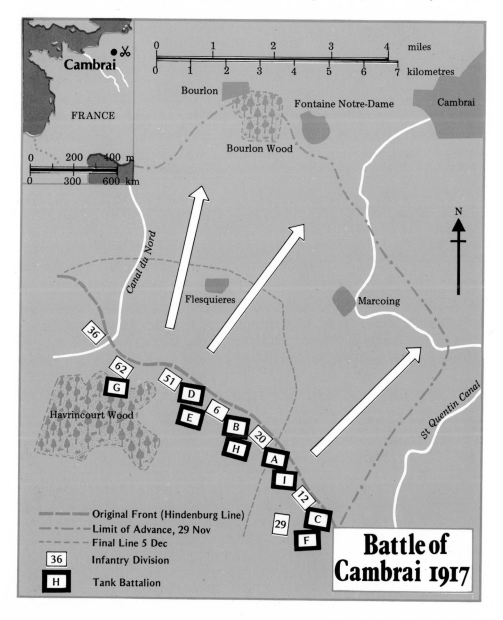

RIGHT The tanks travelled to Cambrai by rail. Each is carrying a fascine, a device made from long faggots and used for lining trenches.

BELOW The tanks had broken through; it was up to the infantry to exploit their victory. A patrol from the North Lancashire Regiment marches into the ruins of Cambrai. But the success did not last long. Ten days later, the Germans recovered all the ground they had lost

a half feet long, and carried a crew of eight (a tank commander, a driver, two men who were responsible for the steering, and four gunners). The forty-six-gallon petrol tank gave it a range of twenty-three miles. What was more, it could negotiate vertical obstacles of up to four feet six inches and trenches up to ten feet wide.

Suddenly the idea that so many people had spurned was important. Haig wanted the landships for use in his forthcoming offensive on the Somme. They must, he stressed, take the enemy by surprise. Security became a problem: the name 'landships' was much too descriptive. Couldn't they be called something else? Since they looked vaguely like tanks, Swinton suggested they be called 'tanks'. The idea was adopted.

The early versions came in two sexes. Male tanks were armed with six-pounder guns mounted in sponsons on the sides of the hull. The females were armed only with machine guns. Both, unfortunately, contained a snag: they were not, as the saying went, splash-proof. In other words, fragments of steel were apt to break off the insides, causing head and face injuries to the crews. As a result, the men were provided with masks. Each had a fringe of chain mail across the bottom to protect the mouth and throat.

Haig must have been desperate. When he first committed tanks to battle, the numbers were too few and the time was too soon. The French treated them in much the manner they might have greeted a circus; the British senior officers hadn't the slightest idea of how to use them. Nor were the machines themselves fully developed: of the forty-nine that set off for the assembly point on 15 September 1916, only thirty-six arrived there. The attack itself scared a number of German soldiers, but there were not enough tanks for the panic to become widespread. At the end of the day, the Commander-in-Chief was compelled to admit that he had made only small gains in return for disproportionately heavy casualties. The tanks, it seemed, had done little to help.

Cambrai was another matter. On 20 November 1917, in the vicinity of a small town forty-five miles south of the Somme, 381 tanks assembled. There was no preliminary barrage, no infantry in support – just the sight of these grey, and to many German eyes terrifying, monsters ambling through the smoke. As an advertisement for this newcomer to warfare, it was magnificent. They crossed three lines of enemy trenches; knocked a hole four

ABOVE The battle is almost over. 'Lusitania' makes her way into a captured village.

OPPOSITE ABOVE *Punch* was jubilant about the success of the tanks. In this cartoon, the role of St George is played by Douglas Haig. Whatever Haig's shortcomings as a commander-in-chief, he had the sense to realize the tank's potential when many senior officers doubted it.

OPPOSITE BELOW One of the spoils of war captured in the fighting at Cambrai was this 9.5-inch German naval gun. It was taken during an early stage in the battle and towed away by a tank.

miles wide in the front; and penetrated to a depth of five miles. All told, ten thousand Germans were accounted for in return for fifteen hundred British casualties. When the news reached London, the church bells were rung to celebrate the victory. It must, people told themselves, mean that the war was nearly over. And then everything turned sour.

The generals still had not learned how to manage tanks. The infantry couldn't keep up with them. The cavalry could, but they thundered into certain death. In the end, the Germans brought up powerful reserves, and the tank attack spent itself. The battle now degenerated into the situation so familiar to the Western Front. Compared with the comparatively modest casualties of the first day, the old familiar pattern of mass death returned. The British losses amounted to 44,207, the German to somewhere between 45,000 and 53,000. As for the penetration made by the tanks, ten days later the Germans recovered all their lost ground and more.

How can a brilliant victory be transformed into a dismal failure? The question became even more pertinent when people remembered that the British had a brand new, and potentially devastating, weapon such as the enemy did not possess. A court of inquiry was held in London to examine the conduct of the battle. The findings reflected the fiasco of Cambrai itself. The responsibility, reported the court, lay with the other ranks and the junior officers. The generals, as was their custom, were pronounced blameless.

Footnote: In comparison with Big Willie, the most powerful tank in the British army today is named the 'Chieftain'. Its top speed on a road is thirty miles per hour, and it carries sufficient fuel to cover two hundred and fifty miles. Manned by a crew of four, it weighs fifty tons. The United States' heavyweight battle tank is referred to as the M47. It is lighter than the Chieftain (forty-four tons), and has a maximum speed of thirty-seven miles per hour. A crew of five operates it. Finally, Russia's biggest tank is the T54. It can reach speeds of up to thirty-one miles per hour, weighs thirty-six tons, and has a range of two hundred and fourteen miles. Like the Chieftain, it is manned by a crew of four.

13 The Rush to Dunkirk

Blitzkrieg 1940

On the night of 9 May 1940 the so-called 'Phoney War' came to an end with the drone of aircraft engines over Holland. For the past seven months nothing very much had happened on the Western Front. The French and British armies had constructed some field defences in an attempt to lengthen the incomplete Maginot Line (a monstrous underground system which for sheer uselessness rivalled the Brontosaurus). The Belgians and the Dutch had looked to their fortifications – but without consulting the Allies for fear of provoking the Germans and thereby jeopardizing their neutrality. As for the German high command, it had filled in the months more profitably by tidying up a plan. If it succeeded, France would fall; the western seaboard of Europe from the tip of Norway to the Spanish frontier would be in German hands; and the doom of Britain would be (or ought to be) inevitable.

In 1940, the German army showed the rest of the world how to use tanks in battle. The lesson was to thrust forward and to keep on thrusting.

Composed by the Chief of Army General Staff, General Franz Halder, and including ideas supplied by Hitler and General von Manstein, it had two main elements. One was to occupy Holland and Belgium; the other was to thrust through the Ardennes, pierce the line of the French army, and then swing round towards the coast. By the invasion of the Low Countries, Halder expected the British Expeditionary Force and a number of crack French units to move forward to Belgium's aid. This would upset the Allied flank; indeed, when this took place, the Germans gave it every encouragement. Almost everywhere else in the campaign, there were punishing attacks by the Luftwaffe. In this instance, there were none.

But the weight of the offensive was to be concentrated in the Ardennes. It was here that the French army was weakest. Many of the troops were elderly reservists; furthermore, the French high command believed that the hills and woods of the countryside would preclude the use of tanks. They were disastrously wrong. It was, perhaps, typical; for the French were still thinking along the lines of the First World War. They were prepared for trench warfare, for battles in which the armoured vehicles were spread out among the infantry, and not concentrated in a fast-moving mass.

The Germans, on the other hand, had conceived a new notion of warfare which had little to do with trenches. Known as *blitzkrieg*, it depended on mobility, on a rapid thrust that slashed a hole in the enemy line. Once this

A Junkers Ju 52, backbone of the German aerial transport fleet, in flight over Holland.

Yesterday, Rotterdam was a peaceful city, secure in a neutral country. Other people might fight wars; the citizens of this Dutch port went about their business in peace. And then, suddenly, Nazi aircraft swooped out of the sky, and bombed the heart out of the city.

had been achieved, the troops poured through. It was non-stop, breathtaking, a concept that did not envisage the possibility of defeat. Superb organization was of course essential, and so was air support, and so was a high standard of morale among the soldiers. In this last respect, the men of the Wehrmacht were very different from the French. They were full of enthusiasm and no less laden with courage. The French forces (or most of them) had been landed with a war they did not really want. Their mobility was sluggish, their weapons out of date, and the tactical skill of their leaders negligible.

On 7 May, the Dutch government had received rumours of an impending attack. A few minutes before midnight on the 9th they were shown to be correct, but this was like nothing that had ever been experienced before. It was not yet a matter of an army hurling itself across a frontier – the peril came from the sky. First of all, dive bombers plunged towards the airfields, releasing their loads of destruction at the last possible moment. Then came airborne troops, some falling by parachute, others landing in gliders, who grabbed key positions and held them until the overland forces arrived. The Dutch airforce was virtually wiped out before its aircraft could get off the ground. By 12 May, advanced German units had linked up with paratroops south of Rotterdam. On the 14th, the Dutch government was sent an ultimatum: unless all resistance ceased immediately, Rotterdam itself would be bombed. The government agreed, but their reply arrived too late. Suddenly, out of a spring sky, fifty Nazi aircraft swooped on the city. There was no opposition, nothing to ward off the deluge of destruction.

Simultaneously, Belgium was overrun. The pride of that country's defence system was a fort named Eben-Emael, situated south of Maastricht at the junction of the River Meuse and the Albert Canal. Hitler himself had worked on the plan for its capture. It was original, and one of the few examples of the Führer's military ideas that did him any credit.

To attack the fortress from the ground might be slow and expensive. There

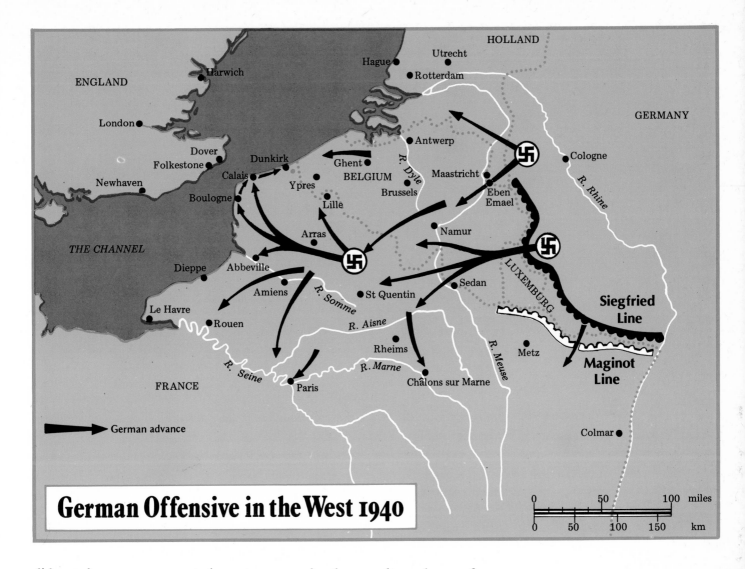

German Offensive in the West 1940

German advance

did not, however, appear to be any reason why the assault need come from this direction. If men equipped with special explosives were landed on the flat roof, the inhabitants would be taken by surprise, and the impact could be devastating. A small team of outstanding airborne troops was specially trained for the project at an old citadel in Czechoslovakia. At half-past five on the morning of 10 May, they made an impeccable landing on top of Eben-Emael in nine gliders (perfect for the undertaking since, being silent, they did not disturb the garrison). Within ten minutes, they had wrought an impressive amount of destruction. When it was all over, their casualties amounted to six killed and nineteen wounded. The Belgians lost about a hundred, and the remainder (eleven hundred) were taken prisoner. Among the dead was the commandant, who committed suicide.

By 11 May, the survivors of the Belgian army had been dislodged from all their strongholds, and had become merged with the French and British forces. But by now a new weapon had been introduced – terror. The suddenness and the severity of the German offensive had been shattering. The dread of air raids produced almost as much panic as the raids themselves. Stories of atrocities, related over the radio, did little to help matters; and everywhere tales were told of parachutists and saboteurs. For a great many Belgian citizens, the only road to safety seemed to be the one that led to France.

The stampede began. Highways became choked with refugees; railway stations were overwhelmed; food shops and petrol dumps were looted. It was as if a nation had gone out of its mind. Naturally, this huge exodus impeded the movement of Allied troops. The Germans, on the other hand, were far from worried. Over in the Ardennes, their surge towards victory was just about to begin.

French generals were numbed by a state of shock. Even Hitler was staggered by the speed of events, the unstoppable dynamic that drove his army on. As Halder noted in his diary, 'Führer is terribly nervous. Frightened by his own success, he is afraid to take any chances and so would rather pull the reins on us.' By the following day, however, he had recovered – which was just as well. Nothing could halt this fantastic assembly of armour that had sliced through the French line and was now heading for the coast. Nothing like it had ever been seen in warfare before.

The key to it was von Rundstedt's Army Group A, supported by three Panzer corps led by General Paul von Kleist. Within them was concentrated the bulk of the German armour (including 2,580 tanks). Indeed, at one point, the column stretched back a hundred miles from the edge of France to fifty miles on the far side of the Rhine. Furthermore, they had more than adequate air support. When, for example, General Heinz Guderian – the star of von Kleist's force – was operating near Sedan, he was able to call upon a considerable strike force to pound the opposition and leave it in shreds. In contrast to the four thousand planes of the Luftwaffe, the French had only a paltry seven hundred. The British, since the bulk of the RAF was assigned to the defence of the UK, could muster no more than two hundred. In the face of such grossly uneven odds, they did not last long.

Fort Eben-Emael on the Belgian frontier near Maastricht was impregnable. Nobody had any doubts about that – until it was captured by a small force of airborne troops, who landed on the roof in gliders. With carefully placed charges of explosives, they put the fort out of action in a way that nobody had dreamed possible.

If there had been a flaw in the German design, it would have been the River Meuse. The French had blown the bridges, and crossing it might have been a problem. But nothing, it seemed, could delay the advance. Two sixteen-ton motor ferries were captured and made to work; rubber dinghies served to get the infantry spearheads across; and once the far bank had been secured it became possible to assemble pontoons.

Kleist's forces hurried on. According to a staff officer serving with the BEF, 'The Germans have taken every risk – criminally foolish risks – and they have got away with it . . . they have done everything that should not be done by orthodox book-trained stereotyped soldiers and they have made no mistake.' The trouble was that the books he referred to had been written for a previous generation of warfare.

By 23 May, the German advance guards were attacking Boulogne and Calais. The BEF had already been cut off: its only hope was that a French army, driving up from the south, would relieve what amounted to a state of siege. By the 26th, it became clear that no such army would come. General Viscount Gort, VC, was advised to fall back to the coast in readiness for an evacuation.

This would have been von Rundstedt's opportunity to annihilate Gort's ten divisions, but the German general paused. According to his account, Hitler was responsible. The Führer had over-estimated the casualties among the tanks and armoured cars – and had taken an over-pessimistic view of the time required to repair them. He also believed that the ground in the neighbourhood of Dunkirk had been flooded and was unsuitable for tank

The last of the refugees have left the Belgian town of Louvain. Now it is almost deserted – abandoned to the German conquerors. All that remain are a few sappers who, presently, will blow up a bridge. Then they, too, will depart.

warfare. As a clincher, he was aware of the fact that the French armies in the south had not yet been destroyed. Rundstedt's army group must remain intact for the march to Paris. In any case, Goering assured him, no attack was necessary: the Luftwaffe could be relied upon to wipe out the BEF.

A couple of days later Hitler changed his mind, but by then it was too late. The BEF and French units had been able to strengthen their defences – sufficiently, at any rate, to keep off the enemy until the evacuation had been completed. Between 29 May and 4 June, 337,131 men were taken off the beaches at Dunkirk in 887 ships and smaller craft.

But the Germans thrust on, and the end of the campaign was very near. On 14 June they reached Paris; by the 17th they had reached the Swiss frontier. That day, the eighty-four-year-old Marshal Pétain, who, in a recent cabinet reshuffle, had been appointed vice-president of the Council, asked for an armistice. It was signed a week later at the exact point in the Forest of Compiègne where the negotiations for the end of the First World War had taken place. On the earlier occasion, a railway restaurant car had been used. On Hitler's insistence, the coach was removed from its resting place in a Paris museum and employed again. The Führer's honour was satisfied at last.

ABOVE The River Meuse should have been a barrier; a ribbon of water, that would at least delay the German Panzer forces. In fact, the crossing was easy – too easy.

OPPOSITE Somewhere beyond the reach of the photographer's camera, German troops are crossing a river. Bombers have already pounded the Allied positions on the far bank, but nothing is left to chance. These infantrymen, armed with rifles and a light machine gun, are covering the operation.

ABOVE The British soldiers wait patiently on the beach at Dunkirk to be evacuated. An armada of 887 ships and boats will take the men – 337,131 of them – to safety.

LEFT German troops advancing through a forest on the Western Front in 1940.

OPPOSITE A German recruiting poster for the Luftwaffe.

143

14 The Final Struggle

The Ardennes 1944

General Sepp Dietricht, whose 6th SS Panzer Army was employed on the northern edge of the German prong. After heavy fighting, one of its divisions reached a range of hills overlooking the River Meuse, but there was no support from the flanks or the rear and before long, it was smashed by the US 2nd Armoured Division.

By the autumn of 1944, the Allied forces – under the command of Dwight D. Eisenhower – were approaching the Rhine along a broad front. As Hitler saw the situation, there was only one hope: to launch a counter-offensive that would break through the Ardennes, and thrust on to Antwerp via Liège and Namur. If it succeeded, its effects would be twofold. It would cut Eisenhower's armies into two; and it would deny him the use of a vital port, on which all his northern forces depended for their supplies.

Hitler and his chief of staff, General Alfred Jodl, began work on the plan in late September. There were innumerable objections. His commanders in the field said it would be almost impossible to retake Antwerp – and utterly out of the question to hold it. The offensive would expend reserves that were essential for the defence of Germany; troops were much more badly needed on the eastern front against Russia; and so on. But Hitler was adamant. The Allied line was weakest in the Ardennes – the operation had every expectation of success. Indeed, his imagination was getting out of control. He foresaw a situation in which the British forces were once more driven to Dunkirk. And this time there would be *no* escape. When eventually orders were issued to von Rundstedt (who was to command the operation), they contained a mass of details – even down to the timing of the various artillery bombardments. Ominously, the words 'Not to be altered' were appended in the Führer's own handwriting.

On 12 December, the commanders received their instructions. The meeting took place in a deep bunker; the generals approached it between two ranks of SS guards, and, before entering, their weapons and briefcases were removed. Hitler was taking no chances: the July assassination plot had nearly succeeded. There would be no second attempt.

The gist of the idea was that three Panzer armies would advance in line abreast. Reading from north to south, they would be General Sepp Dietrich's 6th SS Panzer Army, General von Manteuffel's 5th Panzer Army, and General Erich Brandenberger's 7th Panzer Army. Field-Marshal Walter Model would be in over-all command, under von Rundstedt. A great deal depended on surprise. Consequently security was of the utmost importance. In this instance it was to be carried to the nth degree: it was not intended merely to suppress information, but to distribute, so to speak, false clues.

Lieutenant-Colonel Otto Skorzeny – the uncommonly daring SS officer who had released Mussolini from captivity – was responsible. Men who spoke English exceptionally well were recruited from all the services, given special training, equipped with captured weapons and vehicles, and dressed in American uniforms. Known as *Kommando* Groups, they were divided into two. One (styled the 150 Panzer Brigade) was to support the forward divisions of Dietrich's army and secure the bridges across the Meuse. The other was to be broken down into units of four, each provided with a jeep. Their purpose was to misdirect traffic, spread rumours, change road signs, and generally do everything they could to create confusion.

Much depended on the weather. The ideal would be a fine day to begin with, quickly followed by poor visibility to protect the advance against air attack. The Germans were fortunate. The offensive began on 16 December, and the skies were indeed clear. On the following day, fog set in and very obligingly persisted for eight days. Just as Hitler had hoped, the operation took the Allies by surprise. There had been reports which, if assembled intelligently, would have produced a rough picture of coming events, but they had been treated with scepticism. At this stage in the war, it seemed ridiculous

ABOVE Field-Marshal Walter Model was in over-all command of the Panzer armies.

LEFT General von Manteuffel. His Panzers were at first successful against the Americans.

ABOVE German motorcycle reconnaissance troops, the antennae of the Panzer divisions.

RIGHT Brigadier-General Anthony C. McAuliffe, who commanded the American troops holed up in Bastogne.

to imagine that the enemy was capable of mounting a major attack. Furthermore, bad weather had hampered air reconnaissance – the one thing that would have supplied proof.

The front covered a sector eighty-five miles wide. At first things seemed to be going well for the three Panzer armies. Lieutenant-General Courtney H. Hodges's First Army received the initial impact, when Dietricht's tanks and motorized infantry hurled themselves at v Corps. After three days of heavy fighting, however, only one formation managed to get through. It swept on towards Liège, by-passing Hodges's headquarters at Spa by a few miles and thus missing an opportunity to capture the General himself. On the 19th, it was halted.

Farther south, Manteuffel was more successful. With no preliminary artillery barrage, he smashed into Major-General Troy Middleton's thinly spread VIII Corps; encircled the inexperienced 106 Division on a ridge known as the Schnee Eifel; broke through the 28th Division (under strength at the time); and came within close distance of the important road junction at Bastogne. Troy Middleton was in trouble.

On Manteuffel's left, Brandenberger should have been protecting the southern flank. But his army was the weakest of the three; after coming up against the US 4th Infantry Division and units of the 9th Armoured Division, his instruction to take up defensive positions between Luxemburg and the Meuse became impossible. The formations on the right of his line were the only ones able to keep pace with his neighbour. As for Dietricht, the moment his thrust was halted, the dream of retaking Antwerp crumbled into pieces.

The picture might have been taken in 1940. But the year is 1944, and the prisoners of war are Americans. For them the war is over. Before very long, the German tank crew will also be taken into captivity – or else be killed.

The *Kommando* Groups of von Skorzeny were proving their value – if only to a somewhat limited degree. Of the forty men sent into the field, eight were captured, and later shot. The others got back to Germany. Their list of accomplishments included valuable reports on troop movements, the locations of ammunition dumps and airfields, and the misdirection of an entire US regiment along the wrong road. As an unexpected spin-off benefit, a captured *Kommando* officer expressed the belief that an attempt was to be made on the life of General Eisenhower in Paris. This led to a massive (and unnecessary – there was no truth in the statement) security operation, in which protective troops and decoys were everywhere.

Eisenhower himself had problems enough. The Panzer armies had created a salient and there were no signs to suggest that their energy was spent. Somehow, a force numbering two hundred and fifty thousand men, a thousand tanks, and countless other vehicles, had assembled and embarked on an offensive – unsuspected and unharassed. The persisting fog kept his aircraft on the ground, and his troops had been severely mauled. All attack operations in the direction of the Rhine were suspended. General Patton was instructed to disengage from his advance against the Saar and to hit back from the south. Field-Marshal Montgomery was put in charge of all troops on the northern side. It was as if Model's forces were a tooth, Patton's and Montgomery's the jaws of the dentist's forceps.

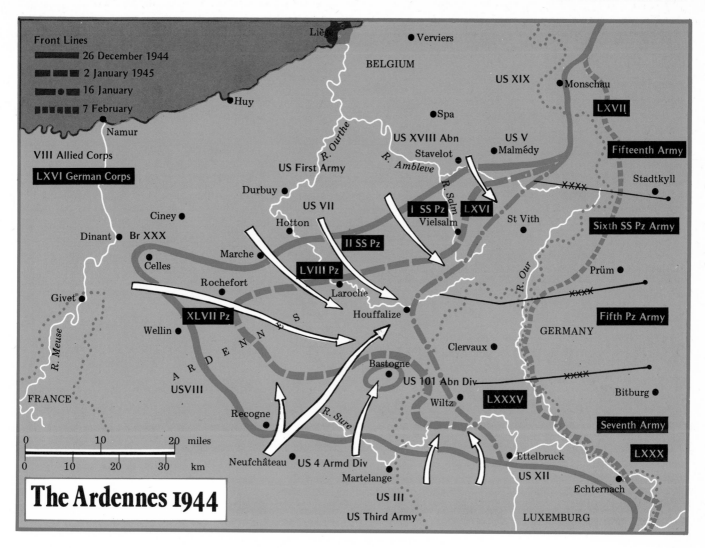

Front Lines

▬▬▬▬	26 December 1944
▬■▬■	2 January 1945
▬▬●▬	16 January
▬■▬■	7 February

VIII Allied Corps

LXVI German Corps

US First Army

Liège

Verviers

BELGIUM

US XIX

Monschau

LXVII

Spa

Huy

US XVIII Abn

US V
Malmédy

Fifteenth Army

Stadtkyll

Namur

Stavelot

R. Ourthe

R. Ambleve

Durbuy

US VII

I SS Pz

R. Salm

LXVI

St Vith

Sixth SS Pz Army

Ciney

Hotton

Vielsalm

Dinant   Br XXX

II SS Pz

Celles

Marche

LVIII Pz

R. Our

Prüm

Rochefort

Laroche

Houffalize

Fifth Pz Army

Givet

R. Meuse

XLVII Pz

GERMANY

Wellin

Clervaux

A
R
D
E
N
N
E
S

Bastogne

Seventh Army

FRANCE

USVIII

US 101 Abn Div

Wiltz

LXXXV

Bitburg

Recogne

R. Sure

LXXX

Ettelbruck

Seventh Army

Neufchâteau   US 4 Armd Div

US XII

Echternach

Martelange

US III

LUXEMBURG

US Third Army

0	10	20 miles
0	10	20 30 km

The Ardennes 1944

Meanwhile, the 7th US Armoured Division was holding on to the key town of Saint Vith, and the 101 Airborne Division was making a desperate stand at Bastogne. At one point, the commander of the encircling Panzers sent his opponent, Brigadier-General Anthony McAuliffe, a demand for surrender. McAuliffe replied with what must be the most succinct communication in the history of warfare: 'Nuts'. As it happened, he was in no position to repel another attack, but it did not matter much. The German force was in no position to make one.

While the rest of Dietrich's army had been forced to stand still, the 2nd Panzer Division had pressed on. By Christmas Eve, it had reached a range of hills overlooking the Meuse. As an achievement taken in isolation, it may have been impressive. Strategically, however, it made less sense; for the 2nd Panzer Division was now on its own, cut off from all assistance from the flanks and from the rear.

On this day, too, the fog, which had served the Germans so well, disappeared at last. Eisenhower's planes were able to take off; and, with the narrow roads crammed with German soldiers and vehicles, there was no lack of targets. The Luftwaffe gave a dying twitch by sending seven hundred aircraft into the sky to attack Allied airfields in France, Belgium and Holland. The German pilots did all·that anyone could have expected of them by destroying two hundred fighters and bombers. But it was not enough. There

OPPOSITE ABOVE By 17 December 1944, the German intentions had become clear to the Allied generals. Everything suggested that they might follow the lines of the 1940 *Blitzkrieg*. Among those present at a hastily convened conference at SHAEF headquarters were (*left to right*) General Omar Bradley, Air Chief Marshal Sir Arthur Tedder, General Dwight D. Eisenhower, Field-Marshal Montgomery, and Lieutenant-General W. H. Simpson.

OPPOSITE BELOW Lieutenant-General Courtney Hodges, whose First Army received the initial impact from the Panzer armies.

were many, many more. Had Hitler realized it, his offensive was doomed from the moment the weather cleared. But Hitler's mind was far removed from the realities of the situation. His armies had driven a wedge between the Allied forces. From tip to base it measured fifty miles, and he intended to maintain it. It was not until 8 January that he sanctioned a limited withdrawal. But by then the situation was far beyond repair.

The tide of battle turned on Christmas Day. The unfortunate 2nd Panzer Division, precariously perched in front of the Meuse, was smashed by the US 2nd Armoured Division. On the following day, the US 4th Armoured

ABOVE Mid-winter. The ground covered with snow. Against this Christmas-card setting, tanks of General Patton's 4th Armoured Division move to the relief of Bastogne.

OPPOSITE Snow helps camouflage US First Army artillery positions.

BELOW After the conflict – the devastated Ardennes landscape.

Division forced its way through to beleaguered Bastogne. In the north, Hodges's First Army began to pound its way through the opposition; southwards, Patton's advance was making excellent progress. The noose around the salient was now complete; it was simply a matter of pulling it tight.

It was now snowing and the roads were covered with ice. Although the 4th Armoured Division had gained the approaches to Bastogne, it had not yet succeeded in reaching the 101 Airborne. With the rest of the German offensive now in disarray, this was the last remaining flaw in Eisenhower's design. What was more, Hitler had ordered Manteuffel to bring up fresh troops. Patton's army and the reinforcements ran into each other on 30 December. The result was a ferocious battle fought in near-Arctic conditions. At the end of it, Patton was, predictably, victorious. The Ardennes offensive was to all intents and purposes dead.

For several months, they have been advancing – pushing everything before them. But suddenly the tide of battle has changed, and these men of the US 34th Infantry Regiment are compelled to dig in. One of them has already been killed by German artillery fire. Others will share his fate.

By 5 January, Hodges had regrouped, and Patton was on the march once more. On the 9th, he left Bastogne behind him and the forceps began to close. Even after the limited withdrawals had been permitted on the 8th, the German forces fought on with the determination of despair. To admit that the offensive had failed was to admit that the war had been lost. Nothing after that could hinder the advance of the Western Allies into Germany. On the 12th, the Russians began their winter campaign; on the following day, Hitler authorized a full scale retreat.

During the next two weeks, Model – with a great deal of skill – extricated his armies from the trap. At the height of the fighting, thirty-three Allied divisions had been set against twenty-nine German divisions. Each side had suffered heavy losses. The score of German casualties amounted to 120,000 men, 600 tanks and assault guns and 1,600 aircraft. The Allies' toll added up to 8,400 killed and a further 69,000 who had either been wounded or were missing. The difference was that these could be replaced; the German gaps could never be refilled.

But scarcely less serious was the effect of the ill-fated offensive on morale at home. This, more than the thousand-bomber air raids, more even than the disastrous situation on the eastern front, made people aware that before very long the war would be over. The prospect of defeat was an unpleasant one. Over a decade ago, Hitler had brought the German people out of some sort of wilderness and inspired them with a dream. The dream now lay in ashes. After a brief snatch of sunlight, another darkness seemed to lie ahead.

Men of US 101 Airborne Division are besieged in the town of Bastogne. On the previous day, German bombers flew over, and there are still casualties lying in the street. It is Christmas Day, but nobody is in a mood to celebrate.

Conclusion

The stories related in this book have accounted for a great many lives. An army goes into battle; it wins or it loses. Either way, thousands (sometimes tens of thousands) of men die. Each death becomes a small part of a large statistic, a fragment of history so minute it is meaningless. But if you're the man the bullet hits, the bomb maims, the shell blows to pieces, it is different. Every battle casualty is a human being; each is a deep personal tragedy. This is something no reader of military history should ever forget.

RG

Acknowledgments

Photographs and illustrations are supplied by or reproduced by kind permission of the following:

Aero Pictorial Library: page 38
Marquess of Anglesey: 35, 39
Boudot-Lamotte, Paris: 13 (*above*)
British Museum: 13 (*below*), 91 (on loan to the Royal Military Academy, Sandhurst), 118–19, 122
Ann S. K. Brown Military Collection: 112–13
Photographie Bulloz, Paris: 77 (*left*), 80 (*right*)
Chicago Historical Society: 104–5
Cooper-Bridgeman Library, London: 127
Cromwell Museum, Huntingdon: 25, 29 (*right*)
John Freeman, London: 61 (*below left*), 64–5, 68
Gettysburg National Military Park: 106–7
Photographie Giraudon, Paris: 81
A. E. Haswell Miller Esq.: 82, 83
Hudson's Bay Company: 34
Imperial War Museum, London: 126, 128, 132, 139, 141, 143
India Office Library, London: 44, 46 (*below*), 48
Collections of the Library of Congress, Washington D.C.: 58, 110 (*above*)
Local History Museum: 125
J. MacClancy Collection: 133 (*below*)
Mansell Collection, London: 33, 47, 88 (*above*)
McCloud Museum, McGill University: 51
Metropolitan Museum of Art, New York: 61 (*above*), 115 (*above*)
Michael Holford Library, London: 8–9, 14–15, 18–19
Musée de l'Armée, Paris: 77 (*right*), 78, 78–9
Musée de Versailles: 70
National Archives, Washington D.C.: 60 (*above*), 114, 115 (*below*), 144, 145, 146 (*below*), 147, 148, 150, 150–1, 151, 152, 153
National Army Museum, London: 30–1, 46 (*above*), 49, 54–5, 61 (*below right*), 65 (*below*), 98, 99 (*below*), 116, 122–3, 123
National Gallery of Art, Washington D.C.: 73
National Gallery of Canada, Ottawa: 59
National Monuments Record, London: 9
National Portrait Gallery, London: 10, 22–3, 26, 29 (*left*), 42, 56 (*left*), 65 (*above right*)
National Trust, London: 56 (*right*)
Orbis Publishing, London: 70–1, 110 (*below*), 135, 138, 142, 143, 146 (*above*)
Phaidon Press, Oxford: 10–11
The Parker Gallery, London: 52, 62–3
Public Archives of Canada: 53
Public Records Office, London: 57
Popperfoto, London: 130, 134, 136, 140
Punch magazine: 133 (*above*)
Radio Times Hulton Picture Library, London: 21, 72, 84, 93, 94–5, 95 (*left*), 97, 100–1, 102–3, 117, 120, 124–5, 130–1
Stadtische Galerie, Landesmuseum, Hanover: 27
Donald Southern: 60 (*below*)

ACKNOWLEDGMENTS

Society for Cultural Relations with the USSR, London: 80 (*left*)
Victoria and Albert Museum, London: 40-1, 74-5, 86-7, 88, 90, 92, 95 (*right*),
    96 and jacket
Virginia Historical Society: 105
Yale University Art Gallery: 66, 69

All possible care has been taken in tracing the ownership of copyright material
used in this book and in making acknowledgment to its use. If any owner has not
been acknowledged the publishers apologize and will be glad of the opportunity
to rectify the error.

Maps drawn by D. P. Press.

Further Reading

Bullock, Alan, *Hitler: a Study in Tyranny* (London and New York, 1952).
Catton, Bruce, *Gettysburg: The Final Fury* (London and New York, 1975).
Cooper, Bryan, *The Ironclads of Cambrai* (London, 1967).
Duffy, Christopher, *Borodino* (London and New York, 1972).
Fleming, Thomas J., *How We are Enemies* (London, 1960).
Fuller, J. F. C., *Decisive Battles of the Western World* (London and New York,
    vol. I, 1939; vol. II, 1955).
Fuller, J. F. C., *The Second World War* (London, 1948).
Green, David, *Blenheim* (London and New York, 1974).
Grey, Elizabeth, *The Noise of Drums and Trumpets* (London and New York,
    1971).
Holloway, W. H., *The Story of Naseby* (Northampton, 1923).
Johnston, H. P., *Yorktown Campaign, 1781* (New York, 1881).
Kinglake, A. W., *The Invasion of the Crimea* (Edinburgh, 1877).
Lemmon, C. H., *Field of Hastings* (St Leonards-on-Sea, 1970).
Merriam, Robert E., *The Battle of the Ardennes* (London, 1958).
Pemberton, W. Baring, *Battles of the Boer War* (London, 1964).
Rogers, H. C. B., *Battles and Generals of the Civil Wars* (London, 1968).
Taylor, Telford, *The March of Conquest* (London, 1959).
Tetlow, Edwin, *The Enigma of Hastings* (London and New York, 1974).
Warner, Philip, *The Crimean War* (London and New York, 1972).
Wilson, C. Holmes, *The Relief of Ladysmith* (London, 1901).

Index

INDEX